THE ORIGINS
OF THE WAR

THE ORIGINS
OF THE WAR

LECTURES DELIVERED IN THE
MICHAELMAS TERM, 1914

BY

J. HOLLAND ROSE, Litt.D.

Fellow of Christ's College and Reader in Modern History
in the University of Cambridge, Corresponding Member
of the Massachusetts Historical Society

Cambridge :
at the University Press
1914

PREFATORY NOTE

I DESIRE gratefully to acknowledge the valuable advice given by the following while the sheets of this volume passed through the Press: Sir Adolphus W. Ward, Litt.D., Master of Peterhouse, J. B. Bury, F.B.A., Regius Professor of Modern History, and J. W. Headlam, M.A., both of King's College, Cambridge. My hearty thanks are also due to the following for help in the arduous task of research: E. R. Adair, B.A., Peterhouse, P. Vos, B.A., Gonville and Caius College, E. la M. Stowell, Corpus Christi College, and Miss Lilian Whitehouse, formerly of Girton College, Cambridge. In so controversial a subject as this, I wish it to be understood that I take sole responsibility for the statements in this volume.

J. H. R.

CAMBRIDGE,
December 4, 1914

CAMBRIDGE
UNIVERSITY PRESS

University Printing House, Cambridge CB2 8BS, United Kingdom

Cambridge University Press is part of the University of Cambridge.

It furthers the University's mission by disseminating knowledge in the pursuit of
education, learning and research at the highest international levels of excellence.

www.cambridge.org
Information on this title: www.cambridge.org/9781107536920

© Cambridge University Press 1914

First published 1914
First paperback edition 2015

A catalogue record for this publication is available from the British Library

ISBN 978-1-107-53692-0 Paperback

CONTENTS

LECTURE I

ANGLO-GERMAN RIVALRY (1875—1888)

Qui trop embrasse mal étreint.
(BISMARCK's favourite motto.)

GERMAN writers often assert that the British Empire is the result of the conscious and persistent effort of our people towards the achievement of World-Empire. We, on our part, believe that Germany has in recent times adopted a World-Policy which, almost of necessity, has brought her into conflict with the British race. Which of the two peoples has of late been the more expansive, the more aggressive, is a question which can be finally and decisively answered only by future historians who have at their disposal documents necessarily withheld from the present generation. But it has seemed to me desirable to try to bring together into these lectures as much evidence as is now forthcoming, for the formation of at least a provisional judgment on this great topic.

At some points, notably as regards the final rupture with Germany, the documentary evidence is fuller than has ever been forthcoming on contemporary events; and we may approach the final stage of our inquiry with a feeling of confidence that the main conclusions are not

likely to be reversed, but only more clearly focussed.
May I also venture to give my experience as to the
completeness and trustworthiness of British official
papers presented to Parliament? After studies in our
archives extending over the best part of twenty years, I
can testify to the honest editing of the Papers presented
to Parliament. In scarcely any case have important
passages been suppressed. Rarely do documents leap to
light that shame the memory of British Ministers, at any
rate since the time of the Younger Pitt. I remember on
one occasion making a remark of this nature to the late
Dr Samuel Rawson Gardiner. I said to him that the
more thoroughly British foreign policy was examined,
the better it came out. He at once replied: "It always
"does; it always does."

I do not propose to discuss here the psychological
question whether there is a radical and incurable hostility
between the North German and the British nature; or
whether a war between their two Empires was inevitable. The former question is too academic for these times:
the second question is futile. A careful study of all the
causes leading to war must, I think, lead to the conclusion
that scarcely any war is inevitable; and that the use of
that epithet is merely a slipshod way of avoiding an examination of all the causes leading to the rupture. No war
is inevitable, unless human passion, folly and blundering
are inevitable; and they are not inevitable unless mankind
is a mere puppet show jerked by blind fate. Let us clear
our minds of all befogging notions. Let us discuss the
evidence; let us seek to understand the characters of the
chief actors, and we shall, I believe, come to the conclusion that this terrible war could have been avoided.

We may leave on one side all the earlier disputes
between Great Britain and Germany. It matters little
now whether Blücher did or did not save us from destruction at Waterloo, as the Kaiser has vauntingly
declared; or that the British Press sympathized keenly
with Denmark in 1864, when she was overwhelmed by
Prussia and Austria; or that certain British steamers
laden with coal for the River Seine were sunk by Prussian
cannon in 1870. All those events belong to a bygone age.
A new order of things came about in 1871, when triumphant Germany became an Empire; and King William
of Prussia became *Deutscher Kaiser* at the palace of
Versailles. Very many of our people rejoiced at the unity
of Germany and the downfall of Napoleon III. No
feeling of security was possible while he was in power.
"Condemned to be brilliant" was the verdict acutely
passed on him by a French thinker; and few persons
believed it possible that a German Emperor would ever
be open to the same charge. The Germans were a
quiet, safe, home-loving people. The French were fickle,
ambitious, dangerous. Central Europe, the weakness of
which had so often tempted the aggression of Bourbon
and Hapsburg, was now secured by the ascendancy of the
House of Hohenzollern. "That Germany is to stand on
"her feet henceforth, and not be dismembered on the
"highway, but face all manner of Napoleons and hungry
"sponging dogs, with clear steel in her hand, and an
"honest purpose in her heart—this seems to me the best
"news we or Europe have had for the last forty years or
"more." Such was Carlyle's verdict after Königgrätz
in 1866; and after Sedan it remained his verdict and that
of very many Britons.

On the other hand, British sympathy with Republican
France, when subjected to the crushing terms imposed
by the victors in 1871, aroused great irritation in Germany.
The tone of Bismarck and the military caste had always
been hostile; and Sir Horace Rumbold testifies to "the
"extraordinary ill-will towards us" which was then manifested[1].

The friction between the two great branches of the
Teutonic family became acute at the time of the war-
panic of the year 1875.   Early in that year the French
Republic gained strength by two important measures.
That of Feb. 25 gave it the beginning of a constitution.
That of March 28 strengthened the army by adding a
fourth battalion to every regiment.   This was enough
for the military party at Berlin.   They did not complain
of those measures.   They complained of the sharp
censures of some of the French and Belgian bishops on
Bismarck's anti-Papal policy.   The Chancellor himself
conjured up the spectre of a Romanist League against
Germany, and uttered these words: "If France does not
"throw over her papal policy, I will not defer making
"war upon her till she is ready; and I know that she will
"be ready in two years[2]."

The frank brutality of this utterance is characteristic
both of the man and of the Junker class whence he
sprang.   His words were echoed in all Prussian newspapers; and a sharp crisis ensued.   German writers have
since endeavoured to minimise the gravity of the situation,
by asserting that the whole affair was a trifle, due to a

---

[1] Sir H. Rumbold, *Recollections of a Diplomatist*, I. 175, II. 297.
[2] Broglie, *La Mission de M. de Gontaut-Biron à Berlin*, pp. 166, 182
(Eng. edit. Part III.).

few hot-heads at Berlin. How misleading this was you will judge if I read a letter from Professor Geffcken[1] to Sir Robert Morier (British envoy at Munich), published in the Memoirs of the latter. After stating that Bismarck was heading towards war, he continues:

> There is to be a great *coup*, and Belgium is the object. I do not say that he is positively bent upon war, because he would be obliged to create a situation where Germany seemed to be the attacked party; and this is not easy, because the Cabinets [of Europe] are cautioned, and there is neither a blind French nor a blind Austrian camarilla pushing to war; but he is resolved to annihilate Belgium, which he declares to be the central government of the political Catholicism, and the heart of coalitional conspiracies. He would easily consent to a partition of that country between Holland and France so that the French might definitely accept the loss of Alsace Lorraine. He speaks contemptuously of England, because it would not be able to give effective military assistance to Belgium.... Might not your Queen write to him [the Emperor William] and tell him plainly what Bismarck aims at and that England can never abandon Belgium ?

The last sentences are significant; for they prove that neither Bismarck nor Geffcken doubted the binding character of our obligation to defend Belgium. Bismarck sneeringly said that we could not save Belgium, if Prussia attacked her; but even he, with his cynical disbelief in the sanctity of treaties[2], did not doubt that we ought to make the attempt. Geffcken, a German constitutional Liberal, took it for granted that we should defend

---

[1] Morier, *Mems.* II. 333. Geffcken (1830–1896) formerly a diplomat, a close friend of the Crown Prince Frederick William, then Professor of Law and Constitutional History at Strassburg (1872–1880). The letter is of March 27, 1875. For the fears of Belgium see *Mems. of Prince Hohenlohe*, vol. II. p. 143 (Eng. edit.).

[2] *Bismarck ; Reflections and Reminiscences*, vol. II. p. 270 (Eng. edit.).

Belgium, as we were bound to do by the treaty of 1839.

Sir Robert Morier believed the danger of a German attack on France to be acute; and two conversations which he had with the German Crown Prince at Munich, did not allay his apprehensions. In fact, the Crown Prince admitted that Moltke badly wanted war[1]. Hostilities would probably have followed but for these saving influences—the peace-loving character of Kaiser William I and of the Crown Prince Frederick William, the intervention of Russia, and the personal appeals of Queen Victoria to Kaiser William I.

On this last topic we have no definite information except that such appeals were made and had the support of the Crown Princess—a fact which accounts for Bismarck's spite against that illustrious lady[2]. Bismarck's letter of Aug. 13, 1875, to the Emperor also shows that Queen Victoria had written to the latter stating that it was easy for her to prove that her apprehensions were not exaggerated. The Queen, therefore, had good authority for believing in a forthcoming attack by Germany upon France[3].

As to the attitude of the British Government little is known. But that little is enough. Lord Odo Russell, then British ambassador at Berlin, informed his brother, Arthur, that Bismarck manifested great irritation with Prince Gortschakoff because of the intervention of the

[1] Sir R. Morier's *Mems.* II. 333–345.

[2] Hanotaux, *Contemporary France*, III. 242: Bismarck, *op. cit.* II. 191–3, 249–253.

[3] *Bismarck; Some Secret Pages of his History*, III. 325–7. Prof. Oncken in the *Cambridge Mod. Hist.* vol. XII. 141, seeks to minimise the incident.

Russian Government on behalf of France, and that shortly afterwards he complained to Lord Odo Russell "of the "preposterous folly and ignorance of the English and "other Cabinets, who had mistaken stories got up for "speculations on the Bourse for the true policy of the "German Government. 'Then will you,' asked Lord Odo, " 'censure your four ambassadors who have misled us " 'and the other Powers'?" Bismarck made no reply[1].

Further, M. Gavard, *chargé d'affaires* at the French Embassy in London, reports that Lord Derby, Foreign Secretary, uttered these words: "Such an act of aggression "(*i.e.* by Germany against France) would arouse in "Europe general indignation, which would nowhere be "stronger than in England. Germany herself would "not brave such a manifestation of opinion.... You may "count on me; you may count on this Government not "failing in its duty. I give you in this matter all the "assurances that can be given by the minister of a con-"stitutional sovereign[2]." Lord Derby went further. He instructed Lord Odo Russell energetically to support the peaceful counsels which the Tsar of Russia was then urging at Berlin. On May 9, M. Gavard met Lord Derby at the diplomatic circle at the Foreign Office, and pressed him for a further statement of his views, because mere moral considerations had never stopped Prince Bismarck. Lord Derby then explained that he spoke of moral indignation, "which forms those Coalitions under "which the first Emperor [Napoleon] succumbed in spite "of all his genius[3]."

[1] Sir M. Grant Duff, *Notes from a Diary* (1886–8), vol. I. p. 129. Bismarck's disclaimers (*Reflections and Reminiscences*, II. 188–193) are obviously insincere.

[2] C. Gavard, *Un Diplomate à Londres*, pp. 242–3.   [3] *Ibid.* p. 246.

In the year 1875 the attack on France desired by the
Prussian military party did not take place, mainly owing
to the urgent representations of the Tsar Alexander II.
At Petrograd he saw the French envoy, General Leflô,
and repeated his earlier assurances that France must be
preserved in a condition of strength. He did more. He
proceeded to Berlin; and after all the world had been
alarmed by Blowitz's revelations made through *The Times*,
he had no difficulty in inducing the Emperor William to
discountenance all thoughts of war[1].

Of set purpose I have avoided details in order to bring
out the salient facts. They are as follows: Whatever
were Bismarck's plans, it is certain that the military
men at Berlin were in earnest in their threats to Paris.
It is also certain that Russia and Great Britain most
urgently reprobated any such threats. Those Governments made it clear that any unprovoked attack by Germany on France would bring about the most vigorous
measures against the aggressor; and that probably all
Europe would take up arms to repel the attack. There
was no formal alliance between Great Britain and Russia
on this question. But they took this course of action
because duty and interest alike prescribed it; and all the
more because Belgium was threatened.

One point more claims attention. The case of 1875 is
well known in Germany All public men, all newspaper
editors, are aware that, from 1875 onwards, it has been
a maxim of Russian and British policy, that France shall
not be suddenly taken at a disadvantage and crushed.
In fact, the German Chancellor, during his memorable
interview with Sir Edward Goschen at Berlin on July 29,

---

[1] H. S. de Blowitz, *My Memoirs*, ch. v.

1914, admitted that to be one of the cardinal points of British policy. The conclusion is obvious. We are bound to conclude that the German expressions of surprise at our intervention in this war are due either to unaccountable ignorance or to a flimsy pretence of ignorance.

The affair of 1875 was very important in many ways. It enabled France to found her Republic and to recover strength; and it created distrust of Germany. The suddenness with which Russia and Great Britain intervened made Bismarck angry at the time and nervous for the future. Evidently his Three Emperors' League, formed in the year 1872, did not count for much when Russia's interests were nearly at stake. He longed for a close union with Russia, and, less so, with Great Britain. Now both *ententes* were uncertain. What wonder that he wrote: "The idea of coalitions gave me nightmares![1]"

Accordingly, he deferred action of all kinds until he could be sure of his ground. Thus, colonial expansion was postponed until after the years 1881–2. Bismarck's views on the colonial question are very remarkable. In 1873 he declared that colonies would be only a cause of weakness, for they could be defended only by powerful fleets, and "Germany's geographical position did not "necessitate her development into a first-class maritime "power....Many colonies had been offered him, but he "had rejected them and wished only for coaling-stations "acquired by treaty from other nations[2]."

Even down to the year 1883 Bismarck continued to discountenance the growing agitation for German colonies.

[1] *Bismarck; Reflections and Reminiscences*, II. 250–3.
[2] Fitzmaurice, *Life of Lord Granville*, II. 337.

But early in 1884 he suddenly veered round, greatly to
the surprise of Lord Ampthill (Odo Russell) and the British
Government. The reasons for this change of front are
probably as follows. In 1882 a number of merchants and
others had founded the German Colonial Society, which
soon set on foot a formidable propaganda. Now, a General
Election for the Reichstag was likely to occur in the autumn
of 1884, the results of which were doubtful; and, as Lord
Ampthill remarked, the cry of "Colonies for Germany"
might be very prejudicial to the supporters of the Chancellor. Thus, according to Lord Ampthill's belief, it was
the nation which led Bismarck to adopt a colonial policy[1].
That fact should be remembered.

Some such departure was natural. For the adoption
of a protectionist régime by Germany in 1879 soon led
to the result generally accruing from such a policy—viz.
over production; and this in its turn led the over-producers
to clamour for new markets where they could sell at
their own prices. Thus Bismarck was logically bound
to take up the colonial policy as a result of his protectionist policy.

On the other hand, I believe that he was by no means
loth to enter on that path; for in 1884 the diplomatic
situation favoured Germany to the highest extent. In
1879 she had framed a defensive alliance with Austria
which decisively checked Russia's forward moves; and,
in passing, we may remember Lord Salisbury's benediction on the Germanic alliance: "To all those who care
"for the peace of Europe and take an interest in the
"independence of nations, I would exclaim 'A crowning
"'mercy has been vouchsafed to the world.'"

---

[1] Fitzmaurice, *Life of Lord Granville*, II. p. 339.

Three years later, this defensive league was strengthened by the accession of Italy. Thus was formed the
Triple Alliance. It is well known that the adhesion of
Italy resulted from her intense annoyance at the seizure
of Tunis by France; and that seizure was first suggested
by Bismarck at the Congress of Berlin[1]. Thus, the same
event busied France in North Africa and strengthened
Germany in Europe. Another event in the year 1882 was
favourable to Germany. British intervention in Egypt
against Arabi Pacha served to embroil us with Turkey.
The Sultan, Abdul Hamid, never forgave us for that
action; and Germany, profiting by his bad temper, soon
began that flirtation with "the unspeakable Turk" which
led up to grandiose schemes in the Levant.

Of those schemes more in the sequel. Here I wish
to point out the extreme caution of Bismarck. He
undertook nothing of moment in the colonial sphere
until he was sure of his position in Europe and saw possible
rivals committed to a forward policy elsewhere; France
and Great Britain in Africa, Russia in Central Asia.
There can be no doubt that he rejoiced at these colonial
adventures; for they led his rivals into spheres remote
from Germany. Bismarck and his underlings knew a
good deal about Russia's policy; for at Berlin on March
24, 1884, he signed a treaty with her and Austria which
in effect revived the *Dreikaiserbund* of 1872. (It was
ratified in the following September at Skiernewice.) For
the present, then, he felt absolutely safe in Europe; and
he probably was aware of Russian plans of expansion
towards India. In November 1884 his able subordinate,
Bucher, said to Busch: "Just keep a sharp look-out on

[1] Crispi, *Mems.* II. 98–109; Blowitz, *My Memoirs*, p. 165.

"the news from Afghanistan. Something will happen
"there soon." Bucher was right. Russia soon annexed
Merv, thereby bringing about sharp tension of feeling
in England, which the Duke of Argyll described as
Mervousness.

Therefore, in 1884, the general situation was peculiarly
favourable to Germany. She had formed a strong alliance,
then the only alliance in Europe. The other Powers
were engaged in centrifugal efforts. Thus Germany could
safely join in the hunt for new markets. We need notice
here only the chief of her enterprises, viz. in South Africa.

There is no doubt that Bismarck and many other
German patriots looked with eager interest at the Boer
Republics of South Africa. The victory of the Boers at
Majuba Hill (Feb. 1881) and the tame surrender of the
Gladstone Government to their demands, spread a deep
impression of the weakness of Great Britain and the
power of the Boers. Nowhere was that impression so
deep as in Germany; and the notion of German supremacy in that part of the world rapidly gained strength.
It was no new programme. Even before the Franco-
Prussian war of 1870, merchants of Hamburg, Bremen
and Frankfurt had urged Bismarck to found a colony in
a temperate climate, and South Africa was suggested.
A scientific expedition set out to view the land, and it
received a warm welcome from President Burgers of
the Transvaal Republic. But their report "was not so
"favourable as to overcome the objections of Prince
"Bismarck," who considered that Germany already had,
as he phrased it, 'too much hay on the fork' "to make any
"large scheme of colonization prudent[1]." In 1875 the

---

[1] Sir Bartle Frere, *How the Transvaal Trouble arose*, p. 258.

programme was changed. A German resident in South
Africa urged on Bismarck the acquisition of Delagoa Bay
from Portugal, with a view to sending a steady stream of
German immigrants into the Transvaal "to secure the
"future dominion over that country, and so to pave the
"way for the foundation of a German-African Empire
"of the future." In that time of doubt and uncertainty
Bismarck did not take up the proposal. But he kept it
before him, with a view to furthering some such scheme
when Germany's position in Europe was better assured.
In 1876 the Boers sent a deputation to Berlin to request
protection from Germany. What passed is not known.
But it is probable that their resistance to Britain's recent
decree of annexation was due, in part at least, to hopes
of assistance from Germany. Probably the Russo-
Turkish war of 1876–7 and the subsequent friction between
Russia and Germany postponed action by the latter;
at any rate Krüger and a Boer deputation which proceeded to Berlin and other capitals, to protest against
the recent annexation by Great Britain, met with no
encouragement[1]. During that time of tension in Europe,
Sir Bartle Frere annexed Walfisch Bay to the British
dominions (1878). There can be little doubt that the
bay had attracted serious attention from the merchants
of Hamburg and Bremen, and that the loss of that
harbour rankled deep.

Early in 1883 the procedure of the German merchants
was as follows. A Bremen merchant, Lüderitz, bought
from a chief a tract of land at Angra Pequeña, a second-
rate harbour some 200 miles north of the Orange River,
and asked the German Government for protection.

[1] *Mems. of Paul Krüger*, p. 145.

14 LECTURE I

Thereupon Bismarck inquired from the British Government whether it would protect Lüderitz. Our Government was utterly callous as to his safety; but it had to consult the Cape Colony about what was behind him. Delays therefore multiplied, and Bismarck became annoyed, because the General Election was coming on, and his enemies would taunt him with weakness unless he scored a colonial success[1]. Finally, Lord Granville declined all responsibility, but declared that annexation of that district by Germany would be an act of encroachment on Her Majesty's rights. At this Bismarck was furious. He resented both the long delay and the somewhat cavalier answer. His son, Count Herbert Bismarck (then at London), had also been nettled by Lord Granville's question whether Germany was not contemplating an extension inland from Angra Pequeña towards the Transvaal. Young Bismarck replied hotly "That is a question of mere curiosity...that does not "concern you[2]." Of course it did concern us very nearly, and his display of temper was more illuminating than the fullest reply.

Finally, a settlement was reached. We needed to buy off German opposition to our occupation of Egypt; and we did so, virtually, by giving up Angra Pequeña and nearly all the coast as far north as the Portuguese possessions. Bismarck was greatly pleased with the surrender. It came just in time to enable him "to bowl over" his enemies in the Reichstag, and the conclusion of the affair produced a most excellent impression throughout Germany—of course exactly the reverse in Cape

[1] Lowe, *Prince Bismarck*, II. 241.
[2] *Bismarck; Some Secret Pages of his History*, III. 120.

Colony, which had annexed that coastline, and now had to witness the reversal of its patriotic act[1]. Thus was laid the foundation of German South-West Africa. Thus began the friction between the British and German Empires in colonial affairs.

Friction was equally acute on the eastern side of South Africa. The chief point in dispute was St Lucia Bay, in the north of Zululand. Germany laid her schemes for securing that bay outright (it was before Tongaland was British). Herr Lüderitz tried to repeat there the same device as at Angra Pequeña, viz. purchase and then a claim for protection. But Germany was too vigorous. She had some dealings with envoys of the Boer Republics[2]; and at the same time she discussed with Portugal the purchase of Delagoa Bay. This was too much even for the long-suffering Gladstone Ministry. Fortunately, it hunted up an earlier purchase of that same land from a former chieftain; and, what was far more important, it sent H.M.S. *Goshawk* to hoist the British flag at St Lucia Bay with an intimation to Berlin that that flag would be kept flying (October 4, 1884)[3].

Even after the annexation of the St Lucia Bay district, a large party of Boers protested against that action and attempted to found there the "New Republic," while the ubiquitous Lüderitz asserted his claim to 60,000 acres in that neighbourhood. When the "New Republic" got into difficulties, Piet Joubert, a Minister of the Transvaal, came thither and suggested that its founders should give

[1] Fitzmaurice, II. 353–5.
[2] *Ibid.* 369. Bucher put down the German failure to Lord Rosebery's sharpness and Count H. Bismarck's want of astuteness (*Bismarck ; Some Secret Pages*, III. 144).
[3] Govt. Blue Book C.-4587, p. 13.

their country to the Germans "on the understanding that "the latter would bring pressure to bear on Her Majesty's "Government to allow of this departure from the Con-"vention." The British Commissioner, hearing of this proposal, reported it to the Home Government, which remained firm. The British flag therefore continued to fly at that important point, despite the annoyance of the German colonial party at the complaisance of Bismarck on this question[1].

Here, then, as elsewhere, German merchants were far more pushing than their Government. But its policy of "peaceful penetration" towards the Transvaal was so far threatening as to cause an important British move in the autumn of the year 1884. Sir Charles Warren was then despatched to South Africa with a small expeditionary force. Strengthened by loyal colonists, it proceeded to Bechuanaland, drove out the parties of Boers who were raiding or half settling that land, and annexed the whole territory to the British Crown. The results were epoch-making. Great Britain secured the highway leading northwards to the Zambesi; and she also drove a solid wedge of territory between the Boer Republics and German South-West Africa. The importance of that success will be obvious if you can imagine German territories coterminous with the Transvaal Republic during the Boer War[2].

Krüger did much to keep open the hopes of the German colonial party. On one occasion he spoke as follows to a party of Germans at Pretoria: "As a child

[1] Govt. Blue Book C.-4587, pp. 87, 91, 110, 119; *Bismarck; Some Secret Pages*, III. p. 144.
[2] For the Bechuana Question see *John Mackenzie*, by W. D. Mackenzie, chs. XI.-XIV; also his articles in the *Contemporary Review* for 1884-5.

"grows up, it requires bigger clothes, the old ones will
"burst; and that is our position today. We are growing
"up, and although we are young, we feel that, if one nation
"tries to kick us, the other will try to stop it....I feel
"sure that, when the time comes for the Republic to
"wear still larger clothes, you will have done much to
"bring it about." The meaning of these words is fairly
clear. The Boer Republics hoped to acquire the whole
of South Africa; and in that adventure they confidently
expected the help of Germany.

In other regions Germany gained enormously. The
Cameroons (1885), German East Africa (1886-1890),
German New Guinea (1884-5), were the three spheres
where she acquired large tracts at the expense of British
firms. Samoa and other islands fell to her later, Samoa
not fully till 1900. In the prosecution of some of these
designs German actions were at times signally un-
scrupulous. The acts of Dr Nachtigal on the Guinea
coast and of Dr Peters in East Africa showed with
what dexterity 'scientific' expeditions could be used for
the purpose of stealing many marches on the British
Government and securing many thousands of square miles
from native chiefs. As a piece of diplomatic cunning, the
revelations of Bucher respecting a German scheme to
seize Zanzibar, are almost unique. It failed only because
the German agent, Rohlfs, bragged about his mission at
Cape Town[1]; and consequently Kirke, our Consul at
Zanzibar, was able to take precautionary measures.
Even so, however, he was unable to save British interests
in the Hinterland, which now forms German East Africa.

---

[1] *Bismarck; Some Secret Pages.* III. 145; *Parl. Papers, Africa,*
No. I. For Samoa see R. L. Stevenson, *A Footnote to History.*

Another curious episode concerns the Kiel Canal. It is not generally remembered that Bismarck was the first seriously to propose the cutting of that canal and the cession of Heligoland by Great Britain[1]. This appears from a Memorandum of Lord Granville in the spring of 1884. Count Münster, the German ambassador at London, broached the subject of Heligoland to Lord Granville in the following terms:

> It was a place of no importance to us in its present state, whereas it would be of immense importance to Germany, to ourselves, and the whole world, if it was made into a good harbour of refuge. This would be an expensive work for us to undertake. We could not be expected to go to such an expense, whereas Germany would be quite ready to undertake it. Prince Bismarck wished to cut a canal into the Baltic, which also would be a great advantage to us as the most powerful nation of the world. But Heligoland, which of course would be always open to our ships, would be a necessary key to such a plan.
>
> Count Münster said it was as good as impossible that Germany and England should ever be at war; but the cession of Heligoland would strengthen the good feeling of Germany towards this country to an extraordinary degree.

Lord Granville here interjected the remark that, doubt-less, the surrender of Gibraltar to Spain would strengthen the good feelings of Spain towards us in an extraordinary degree. After this damping comment, Count Münster was more reserved, and begged Lord Granville not to mention the matter to any of his colleagues.

There, then, the affair ended for the present. But,

[1] He proposed the canal in 1873, but was successfully opposed by Moltke and the military party. *Bismarck ; Reflections and Reminiscences* (vol. II. pp. 32–4). The scheme met with more favour in 1885 (*ib.* p. 34). On the value of Heligoland to Germany see Count Reventlow, *Deutschlands auswärtige Politik* (1888–1913), pp. 44–9.

in recent times, William I and Bismarck, not the present
Kaiser, originated the notion of the Kiel and North
Sea Canal. That Bismarck shrouded the scheme with a
philanthropic glamour, and, with the same specious
professions, sought to wheedle us into the cession of
Heligoland, only marks his sense both of the gullibility
of the British public and of the good nature of Lord
Granville[1]. In this case he somewhat overshot the mark.

It is worth noticing that the colonial expansion of
Germany occurred at a time when she had no fleet adequate
to cope with the British fleet. In truth, the British
Government, both that of Mr Gladstone and that of
Lord Salisbury, looked upon that expansion as a natural
and commendable development. Mr Gladstone went so
far as to utter these words of benediction: "If Germany
"is to become a colonising Power, all I can say is, God
"speed her. She becomes our ally and partner in the
"execution of the great purposes of Providence for the
"advantage of mankind. I hail her in entering upon
"that course, and glad will I be to find her associating
"with us in carrying the light of civilization, and the
"blessings that depend upon it, to the more backward
"and less significant regions of the world." Mr Joseph
Chamberlain, though less benevolent, was equally specific.
On January 5, 1885, he said—"If foreign nations are
"determined to pursue distant colonial enterprises, we
"have no right to prevent them"; but he added that
we would protect our colonies if they were seriously
menaced[2].

[1] See Prince Hohenlohe's *Memoirs* (Eng. edit.), II. 311: "Gladstone
may remain in office. It will be good for us, bad for England" (Nov. 2,
1884).

[2] *Mr Chamberlain's Speeches* (1914), I. p. 136.

Lord Salisbury also was friendly to Germany, regarding her as a possible check on Russia[1].   After 1886 she became so to some extent, a fact which probably explains the extreme complaisance of the Salisbury Cabinet to that of Berlin in 1890.

This topic must be dealt with later.   Here I have sought to show that the German mercantile class pushed on its Government to a colonial policy; that Bismarck (the incarnation of prudence after 1875) entered reluctantly on that new and doubtful path; and that German colonial aims met with no opposition from Great Britain, except where her vital interests were at stake.

[1] *Bismarck ; Some Secret Pages.* III. 143.

LECTURE II

THE KAISER

Principes pro victoria pugnant, comites pro principe.
(TACITUS, *Germania*, ch. 14.)

AMONG no people has the leader and ruler counted for more than among the Germans. With them personal influence has prevailed over the dictates of law and of a constitution. Tacitus noticed that peculiarity among the ancient Germans. In the tribal assembly the chief carried his proposal more by his individual influence than by the authority of his office. So also in *Beowulf*, the chief is the designer of plans, the comrades are merely his followers, led by his forethought, nerved by his example, and rarely, if ever, questioning his decision.

The same is true of recent times. The Great Elector and Frederick the Great made Prussia. Under the two unwarlike successors of Frederick, the Kingdom declined in strength and, in fact, nearly perished, until Blücher and Gneisenau arose to lead the Prussians once more to victory. The contrast between that "King Waverer," Frederick William IV, and the victor of Sedan, William I, is startling; but look at the trio surrounding Kaiser William—Bismarck, Moltke, Roon—and the riddle is solved. In ordinary times the German is home-loving,

passive. Under a great leader he displays the old
Berserkir rage.

This dependence of Germans on their leaders may be
explained thus. Their geographical situation was weak;
for they had no well-defined natural boundaries. Therefore a vigorous lead had to make up for the lack of natural
advantages. Also their laws and institutions were never
thoroughly Romanized. Accordingly, until a recent
time the Germanic State has been weak, and the idea of
law has not dominated life as it has among the Latin
peoples. The Germans have therefore depended more
than any people on their great men. On the appearance
of an inspiring leader, their docility is phenomenal.

In the present age, a leader, who is also ruler, has called
forth to utmost tension all the energies of the German
race. He has accomplished this feat, owing to the conditions of German national life and the charms of his
personality.

His character is more complex and enigmatical than
that of any sovereign of our time, indeed, since that of
the first Napoleon. There are very diverse strains in
his nature. Its basis is Hohenzollern; and he seems to
have forced to the front this side of his being; for he is a
man of strong will-power, as nearly all the Hohenzollerns
have been. Occasionally, as in the case of Frederick
William II (1786–1797) there have been sovereigns
remarkable for love of vicious pleasures; but in the main
the Prussian Kings have worked hard and lived simply.
They have been energetic Commanders-in-Chief, not
remarkable for width of view or variety of attainments.
Macaulay has thus trenchantly described Frederick
William I, father of Frederick the Great: "The business

"of life, according to him, was to drill, and to be drilled.
"The recreations suited to a prince were to sit in a cloud
"of tobacco smoke, to sip Swedish beer, to play back-
"gammon for three half-pence a rubber, to kill wild
"hogs, and to shoot partridges by the thousand." The
Macaulay touch is always too staccato. Still, it is true
that the life of the old Hohenzollerns was rough, almost
boorish.

There were, however, two prominent exceptions—
Frederick I (1688–1713) and Frederick William IV (1840–
61). The latter, the great-uncle of the present Kaiser,
was a man of varied attainments; and to him we must
pay attention; for it is clear that the Kaiser inherits, in
the main, two sets of tendencies. The former of these is
derived from his grandfather, William I (1861–1888), a
man of simple, rigid, and yet not unkindly nature, of
the usual Prussian type; while his predecessor, his
brother, Frederick William IV, was a man of singularly
versatile genius, but utterly deficient in steadfastness of
aim. In conversation he pleased, in action he disgusted,
everybody. Quick to speak, overflowing in ideas, romantic in his outlook on life, he was the ornament of every
social circle, but the despair of every Cabinet. That
cosmopolitan statesman, Baron Stockmar, saw him
during a royal visit to the British Court in 1842 for the
purpose of acting as godfather to His late Majesty,
Edward VII. In a confidential interview the King
exhibited his powers of speech and his restless ambition.
During an hour he dilated on the precarious position of
Belgium. He felt certain that, in case of a Franco-
Prussian war, France would at once seize the Belgian
fortresses. Even in time of peace, he said, Belgium

tended to gravitate towards France. This was dangerous for Germany, and, as the natural protector of Germany, he suggested that the best course of action for Belgium would be to enter the Germanic Confederation. He set forth his views enthusiastically and eloquently, and seemed somewhat surprised when Stockmar maintained that Belgium was resolved to uphold its independence. Stockmar found him a man of sentiment, poetical, inclined to mysticism, a dreamer in politics, and by no means a statesman[1].

In fact, his lack of statesmanship was always apparent. Thus, after instituting a Prussian United Landtag in 1847, he read it an extremely irritating lecture at the opening Session—They were not representatives of the people. He derived his kingly authority from God alone, and he would never allow a sheet of paper (*i.e.* a constitution) to come between "the Lord God in Heaven and his subjects." The same thought led him to reject the crown of a democratic German Empire founded in 1849. He referred scornfully to the new imperial crown as "the iron fetter "by which the descendant of four and twenty sovereigns, "the ruler of 16,000,000 subjects, and the lord of the "bravest and most loyal army in the world, would be "made the mere serf of the Revolution."

This unfortunate King possessed many fatal gifts. He frequently wove plans which it was beyond his power to carry out; for he let his faculties run hither and thither and never concentrated them on one practicable object. After seeing all his plans miscarry, he, in the year 1857, showed symptoms of lunacy; and the last four years of his life were marked by hopeless madness.

---

[1] *Mems. of Baron Stockmar*, ii. pp. 78–85.

His younger brother, William I, was far less imaginative and sensitive. A plain man, who never saw far ahead, he often made mistakes; but, as he never talked much, no one saw that they were mistakes; and he generally had the good sense to retrace his steps before it was too late. After his death, in 1888, Bismarck went so far as to say of him: "When anything of importance "was going on, he usually began by taking the wrong "road; but in the end he always allowed himself to be "put straight again[1]."

Now, that is literally true at many points of his career. Probably his reign would have ended in disaster but for the singularly able guidance of Bismarck and his co-adjutors. We must, however, add that Kaiser William I had a good eye for character; and when he found a trusty counsellor, he never dismissed him, however trying the times. He supported his Ministers steadfastly; and he himself ran straight towards a well defined goal. Distrusting his own abilities, which were slight, he hearkened to good counsel; and therefore the reign of that plain, unassuming soldier ended amidst a galaxy of glory.

Striking the mean between the two brothers, we should arrive at an interesting compromise—a man restless in habit and romantic of speech, yet also possessing great power of organization; a weaver of daring schemes, yet also patient and persistent in preparing for their execution; an orator, yet also a man of action; a lover of the arts, but pre-eminently a soldier. Such a man is Kaiser William II.

He is, I believe, an example of atavism, that is, his nature recurs to that of the previous generations. In few

---

[1] *Bismarck ; Some Secret Pages*, III. 176.

traits of his character does he resemble his father or
mother, except in fondness for literature, art, and music;
and those characteristics he shares with his great-uncle.
As is well known, his mother, formerly Princess Royal of
Great Britain, was very clever—far too clever for the
Prussian Court of her days; and her sharp ironical
remarks, no less than her decidedly English ways, often
brought her into difficulties. Further, the almost democratic views of the father, the Emperor Frederick, were
extremely unpopular in Court circles, witness the brutal
remark of Busch, after his death, at his relief of the
removal of that "incubus."[1] Such was the general feeling
among the governing classes; and the present Kaiser
seems to have displayed very little filial affection during
the long drawn-out agony of that winter and spring of 1888.

With his mother he had previously been on strained
terms owing to her rather too open expression of progressive views and her fondness for England. His
annoyance came to a head, early in the year 1888, owing
to the ardent love of his sister, Victoria, for Prince
Alexander of Battenberg, a noble and chivalrous character,
beloved by nearly everybody except his uncle, the Tsar
of Russia. Because that marriage would have offended
the Tsar, besides introducing one more ally of England
into the Court circle, the present Kaiser and Bismarck
bitterly opposed it. The Empress Victoria no less firmly
advocated it; but, finally, for reasons of State, she and
her daughter had to give way. Bismarck's Journal shows
that it was our Queen, who, during a visit to Berlin,
counselled the surrender of the happiness of her grand-
daughter in order to restore peace in the Imperial family

[1] *Bismarck; Some Secret Pages*, III. 190.

at Potsdam. Queen Victoria did more: she brought about a reconciliation between Prince William and his mother. There, doubtless, is the reason for the veneration which he has always felt for the Queen-Empress. Her death in 1901 inaugurated a period of greater strain between Great Britain and Germany. At this point, again, the atavism of his nature is well marked; and this peculiarity, together with the special reason for gratitude to his grandmother, acted as a check on his anti-British feelings. How strong they were may be judged by a trifling incident. On one occasion his sister, Victoria, talked about being "at home" in England. At once he flung at her an epithet which is semi-officially reported to have been either "goose" or "sheep."[1]

Opposition to parents and to brothers and sisters is often a trait of very decided natures; and it was therefore traditional in the House of Hohenzollern, which is nothing if not decided and determined. We think of Frederick the Great in his youth, caned, starved, and once all but shot, by his bullying father. And the course of the Hohenzollerns has generally been one of sharp zigzags during successive reigns. The revolt of the present Kaiser against the peaceful and progressive tendencies of his father early became evident. He was always a soldier. At the age of eight he exacted a military salute from a somewhat negligent sentinel[2]; and at the age of 23 his portrait was thus limned by Bismarck: "He "wishes to take the Government into his own hands: he "is energetic and determined, not at all disposed to put

---

[1] *Bismarck; Some Secret Pages*, III. 184, 188. M. Harden, *Monarchs and Men*, pp. 16, 99.

[2] Maurice Leudet, *The Emperor William at home* (Eng. edit. p. 27).

"up with parliamentary Co-regents—a regular Guardsman.
"Perhaps he may one day develop into *le rocher de bronze*
"of which we stand in need."   A little later the Chancellor
received from the young prince a curious present—his
portrait with the ominous words written underneath—
"Cave, adsum[1]."

The groundwork of the Kaiser's character is therefore
stiffly and aggressively old-Prussian.   Apart from his
artistic leanings, he exhibits a recurrence to the earlier
type.   His patriotism is intense, almost furious; and
therein lies the secret of his power.   He has evoked a
storm of patriotic fervour such as the world has not seen
for a century past.   Against such a man it is childish
merely to rail.   To insult him is far worse.   Our duty
should be to try to understand him; to find out the
secret of that influence which he has exerted upon his
people; to absorb the best elements of German national
strength into our more torpid and ill-organized society.

Firstly, then, let us notice his phenomenal activity.
He is one of the hardest workers in that nation of hard
workers.   By example, as well as by precept, he requires
the utmost amount of efficient toil in every grade of life;
and the motive everywhere is the same: it is for the
Fatherland.   Germany tolerates no drones.   The hive
swarms with workers; and sport, though it has gained
ground of late, does not absorb the large, the dangerously
large, share of the nation's energies which it unfortunately
does in these islands.   In Germany the welfare of the
nation comes first, the pleasure of the individual comes
second; and neither the Kaiser, nor the public opinion

---

[1] "Take care: I am near you."   M. Harden, p. 96; *Bismarck; Some
Secret Pages*, III. 56.

which he has trained, would tolerate, in times of grave
national crises, the holding of great football matches for
the sake of the gate-money which they bring in. The
Kaiser's career has been a constant appeal for national
efficiency; and hence the prodigious strength which
Germany is now putting forth.

Kaiser William could not have exerted his phenomenal
influence, had he not been endowed by nature with
considerable personal charm. After the reign of the
stiff and severe William I, and the concentrated tragedy
of the three months' reign of Frederick III, the advent of
the young War-lord was hailed with enthusiasm. His
bearing betokened the guardsman, his varied accomplish-
ments dazzled the Court, his words set the blood tingling.
He resembled Henry V after the cautious Henry IV, as
limned by Shakespeare:

Ely.   We are blessed in the change.
Cant. Hear him but reason in divinity,
        And, all-admiring with an inward wish,
        You would desire the King were made a prelate.
        Hear him debate of commonwealth affairs
        You would say it hath been all in all his study:
        List his discourse of war, and you shall hear
        A fearful battle rendered you in music:
        Turn him to any cause of policy,
        The Gordian knot of it he will unloose
        Familiar as his garter.

Here is a very favourable account of the Kaiser
penned by the late Mr Edward Dicey, just before the
State visit to London in the spring of 1911.

No one can be in his company for long without feeling the charm
of his presence and learning something of the breadth of his mind.
He seems to be able to converse on anything, and to converse equally

well on all subjects; nor is the knowledge he shows superficial.
He always goes to the root of the question; and it would be unwise
for anyone not armed at all points to seek an audience with His
Imperial Majesty. He talks quite openly, and in a way which gives
confidence; and he quickly turns from one subject to another
just as the conversation leads him. Courteous and kind, he makes
you feel at home at once; and, while his bearing and mien command
respect, he in no way demands homage[1].

This natural and impulsive manner he inherited from
his mother, who could rarely resist the temptation of
saying a clever thing. But there again the Kaiser's
eloquence and love of oratory is akin to that of his great-
uncle. He is one of the ablest impromptu speakers of
his Empire. Two examples of his art must suffice. In
November 1901 at a meeting of the Institution of Naval
Architects in Charlottenburg he was present at a lecture
followed by a discussion. At the end of the discussion,
to the utmost surprise of the audience, he rose from his
seat, and, ascending the rostrum, delivered a speech
which well summed up the whole of the question in
debate. Never losing himself in technicalities, he made
the question live, lightening it once with a touch of
humour[2].

The other occasion was even more remarkable. It
occurred during a festivity at the University of Berlin.
Arndt's patriotic song of 1813,

> " Der Gott der Eisen wachsen ließ,
>   Der wollte keine Knechte,"

had raised enthusiasm to a high pitch, and that enthusiasm bore the Kaiser to the rostrum. The opening
sentences were somewhat forced and nervous; but his

[1] *The Empire Review*, May, 1911.
[2] L. Elkind, *The German Emperor's Speeches*, pp. 251–3.

will soon banished all nervousness. The full, sonorous
voice began to fill the great hall and dominate the
situation, until at the end the audience spontaneously
burst forth into the patriotic song— "Heil dir im Sieger-
kranz[1]."

Kaiser Wilhelm possesses the imaginative gifts which
add dignity to oratory. His love of Germany's richly
storied past enriched the speech which he delivered in
1902 at Aix-la-Chapelle, the city of Charlemagne. After
dwelling on those historic associations, he launched out
on a wider sphere.

So powerful and so great a figure was that mighty Germanic
Prince, that Rome herself offered him the dignity of the Roman
Caesars, and he was chosen to enter upon the heritage of the
Imperium Romanum—assuredly a splendid recognition of the
efficiency of our German race, then entering on the stage of history.
...But to unite the office of the Roman Emperor with the dignity
and burdens of a Teutonic king was a task beyond the power of man.
What he, with his mighty personality, was able to accomplish, fate
denied to his successors; and in their anxiety to gain the Empire
of the World, the later Imperial dynasties lost sight of the German
nation and country[2].

Would that Kaiser William had learnt that lesson!

There is in his nature a decided vein of romanticism.
It appears in his love of old German literature—its sagas
and mythology. As an instance of the Kaiser's skilful
handling of Norse mythology for the furtherance of his
maritime designs, let me cite part of his speech at the
launching of the ironclad, *Heimdall*, at Kiel in 1892:

We are now called upon to give the ship a name. Its name
will be taken from the earliest history of our forefathers in the

[1] Lamprecht, *Der Kaiser* (Berlin, 1913), pp. 74–6.
[2] *Ibid.* p. 71.

north. Thou shalt receive the name of the god to whom was
entrusted, as his main function, the duty of defence: of that god
whose bounden duty it was to protect and keep the golden gates
of Walhalla from every base intruder. As the god, when danger
was afoot, blew a far-sounding blast on his golden horn and sum-
moned the gods to battle in the twilight of the gods, so may it be
with thee. Glide down into thy element. Be thou ever a faithful
warden of the seas....And if ever the day comes when thou art
called upon to do battle, deal destruction and devastation in the
ranks of thy enemies[1].

A ruler whom the gods wish to destroy they endow
with eloquence. It is a fatal gift, especially in a continental potentate. In the main, the successful monarchs
have been plain, tactful, silent men. From the time of
Maximilian I to that of Napoleon the Great, and down to
William II, rhetoric has kindled enthusiasm in the people,
but it has also alarmed neighbouring Powers. Never
has it been more fatal than with Kaiser William. A
careful and sympathetic observer admits that he
"becomes intoxicated with his own words[2]." This is
undoubtedly the case; and during many years all peace-
loving Germans trembled when it was rumoured that
the Emperor was about to speak or had fired off a political
telegram. Finally, his Chancellor had to insist that both
speeches and telegrams should be subjected to some
measure of official supervision. After that, Europe was
much duller during many a long month.

His worst enemies admit that he is a very interesting
man; and, like the great Napoleon, he hides under a
pleasing surface that reserve of strength which, by

---

[1] Elkind, p. 257.
[2] As at Döberitz in 1903 (Lamprecht, *ibid.* pp. 69–77).

imposing respect and a certain secret fear, doubles the present witchery. A sharp nod of the head, a flash of the eye, a ring in the tone of the voice, and you are reminded that under feline charm lies feline hardness.

For the stern Hohenzollern nature is there, enriched though it was by the Guelph-Coburg strain. Those old Hohenzollern Electors and Kings, who thrashed their sons and dragooned their subjects, bequeathed to him a nature which no civilian training could wholly modernize. Kaiser William's parents had sought to bend his nature towards industrial and economic studies, and therefore sent him to school at Cassel, with an instruction that the artistic side of his nature was to be developed. He was to visit museums, factories, and mines[1]. He would have none of them. There and at the University of Bonn his chief interest was in the army and navy. At Bonn his student's room was full of photographs of German warships, the description of which he knew by heart. Voyages of adventure and discovery were his favourite study; and he longed to visit Egypt[2]. By way of preparation, perhaps, for that visit, he encouraged the fighting spirit among the students. M. Amédée Pigeon, who knew him well at Bonn, writes of his passion for witnessing the students' sword-duels: "He would stand "for an hour around the combatants. How often have "I seen him pale, nervous, attentive, watching the "play of the duellists....He was happy in witnessing "those spectacles where blood flows, where often a bit "of a nose or a cheek is taken off by the sword,...and his

[1] G. Hinzpeter, *Kaiser Wilhelm II* (Bielefeld, 1888).
[2] Leudet, ch. II.; Reventlow, pp. 57–65, 100–2, "Reichsgewalt ist Seegewalt und Seegewalt Reichsgewalt."

"pleasure was redoubled in eluding the police, who are
"supposed to discountenance these duels,...but who, in
"fact, tolerate and wink at them[1]."

Everyone agrees that he was always extremely self-
willed. Even his tutor, Hinzpeter, in an almost official
panegyric, admits that, while outwardly obedient to
University discipline, he went his own way entirely in
the mental domain—witness the following. His first
tutor in matters religious belonged to the progressive
school; but he was suddenly replaced by an extremely
orthodox tutor. The change made no difference whatever
to the pupil's religious beliefs[2]. The incident does not
necessarily prove imperviousness at all parts of the
brain; but it may be taken as symptomatic.

A man possessed of great will-power and personal
charm can generally dominate others; and the Kaiser
has exercised a uniquely fascinating and controlling
power over the German people. As an American writer
has said, wherever you touch the German people, you
touch the Kaiser[3]. Here we may cite as witness one
of the most prolific and patriotic of the German professors. Dr Lamprecht of Leipzig has written the most
careful and life-like study of the Kaiser that has yet
appeared. It was founded on personal knowledge, and
on information procured from the men about him. It
contains two companion portraits, one drawn in 1901,
the other in or just before 1913. A desire for exactitude,
with which there were doubtless mingled considerations
of a prudential nature, led Herr Lamprecht to submit
the former effort to his illustrious sitter; and it was

[1] Leudet, ch. 21.　　　　[2] G. Hinzpeter, pp. 6–7.
[3] P. Collier, *Germany and the Germans*, p. 106.

approved. The picture may therefore be regarded as a full-length royal portrait of the standard Royal Academy type.

Lamprecht lays great stress on the Kaiser's powers of persuasion. He writes: "When one listens to Min-"isters, one is again and again amazed at the extent to "which they merely repeat the Emperor's ideas; and "whoever has seen opponents coming from an interview "with him must have been equally struck by the way in "which they were dominated by the charm of his person-"ality, at all events so long as the immediate effect of "his words lasted."

Professor Lamprecht points to certain defects in the Kaiser's character. He instances his impulsiveness, his hasty resolves and his everlasting restlessness[1]. He also remarks on the curious dualism of the Kaiser's nature; that reason and ambition are pushing him forward to daring enterprises; that sentiment and family associa-tions link him with the past. This is undeniable. An-cestor-worship the Kaiser carries almost to Chinese lengths. He calls his grandfather's palace in *Unter den Linden* "a sacred spot." He speaks of "the sacred feet" of that Emperor, and asserts that William I, if he had lived long ago, would have been canonized, and pilgrims would have come to pray to his bones[2].

As to the Kaiser's religion, the professor does not say much; and it is peculiarly difficult now to dilate on that topic without generating irrational heat. It is well, however, to remember that Kaiser William I was a pious man; but his piety was coloured by his early associa-tions and ingrained ideas. It was a compromise between

[1] Lamprecht, pp. 32–3.   [2] *Ibid.* pp. 39–40.

Christianity and Prussian militarism. Outwardly, he professed the creed of the New Testament; but his guiding spirit was that of the Old Testament—the Prussian army was the chosen people in arms, smiting the Canaanites hip and thigh. In one of his last public utterances he said to the present Kaiser: "If ever a "Government was visibly directed by Providence, the "German Government has been during these late years." That is the feeling also of the grandson. His Christianity has somehow stopped short at the Book of Kings.

In hazarding this statement, I am in general agreement with Professor Lamprecht, who asserts that the Kaiser's religion is of a primitive type, and has its roots in ancestor-worship. There is much of truth in this statement. Indeed, a loyal subject of the Kaiser has set on foot an ancestor hunt and has compiled volumes containing descriptions of 2096 of them.

As we shall soon see, the Kaiser's conception of the future state is that of a kind of Walhalla, where his ancestors occupy the foreground and anxiously watch his exploits. Lamprecht admits that at Potsdam the Christian Deity figures as the Lord of Hosts, whose kingdom must be extended as far as the bounds of the yellow races[1].

Evidently, then, religion and *Weltpolitik* merge into one another and become almost convertible terms. The close connection between them was clear in the year 1897, when the murder of two German missionaries in Kiao-Chao led to the immediate seizure of that important district.

The importance of religion as an instrument of govern-

[1] Lamprecht, p. 42.

ment has never been more frankly stated than by the
Kaiser. The following words to recruits are an example:
"He who is not a good Christian is not a good Prussian
"soldier; and in no circumstances can he fulfil what is
"required of a soldier in the Prussian army." Again:
"Your duty is not easy: it demands of you self-control
"and self-denial—the two highest qualities of the Christian;
"also unlimited obedience and submission to the will
"of your superiors." And again: "As I, Emperor and
"ruler, devote the whole of my actions and ambitions to
"the Fatherland, so you must devote your whole life
"to me[1]." He is excited by martial display and large
assemblies; and it is confidently affirmed by Germans
that too much importance need not be ascribed to his
after-dinner speeches[2]. In short, his temperament is at
times almost neurotic. The symptoms of that nature
are perhaps due to a disease in the ears which at one time
seemed serious. Some sixteen years ago, Dr Bucheron, a
French specialist, wrote concerning this complaint, that
it could be cured partially but never completely eradicated.
In an acute form it caused excessive irritability, which
manifested itself in outbreaks of rage, with relapses into
gloom. Another symptom of the disease was lack
of due affection for parents[3]. Whether this furnishes
the explanation for the peculiar conduct of the Kaiser
in 1888, I will not venture to say. Perhaps that unfilial
conduct had its roots in an instinctive physical repulsion.
Both his parents died of cancer.

[1] Lamprecht, p. 43.
[2] W. von Schierbrand, *Germany: the Welding of a World-Power*
(London, 1902), p. 19.
[3] M. Leudet (Eng. edit.), p. 55. Even Hinzpeter (p. 8) says he was
accused of heartlessness and obstinacy.

Outwardly the Kaiser appears a strong and healthy man; and he seems to have recovered from the ear trouble. But there is certainly something wrong with him, as, for instance, his excessive liability to catch cold. The question arises whether his ailments, be they mental or physical, do not account for the peculiarities of his conduct. His actions, both in private and in public, display an almost febrile restlessness. It is an open secret that he often takes morphia, doubtless in order to procure intervals of calm for himself and his subjects. But the restless symptoms recur, and drive him forth to review garrisons, inspect ships, make speeches, and act as a general stimulus to the world. Professor Lamprecht asserts that the Kaiser becomes calmer in crises, and that those who know declare that he will show himself at his best in great emergencies[1]. That remains to be proved.

A restless nature is nearly always self-assertive; and a self-assertive ruler is certain to be an autocrat. Louis XIV and Napoleon never uttered more autocratic dicta than the Kaiser. Witness these: "One only is "master within the Empire, and I will tolerate no other." "Those who oppose me in my work I will crush" (March 5, 1890). "My course is the right one, and I shall continue "to steer it" (Feb. 1892). In 1893 to the recruits: "There is but one law and that is my law." Finally, under his portrait presented to the Ministry of Public Worship at Berlin he wrote the motto: "Sic volo, sic "jubeo."

His son takes after him in this respect. Hence the opposition to parents, traditional in the House of

[1] Lamprecht, p. 72.

Hohenzollern, is once again acute; and the imperial palace has been the scene of open quarrels, often followed by the departure of the Crown Prince for the sake of health, and, in one instance, by his transference to a distant garrison town. It may, perhaps, finally transpire that the crisis of last July ended fatally owing to the interference of that hot-headed young prince.

From the outset, the autocracy of the Kaiser was seen to be a danger to the peace of the world. His first proclamation to the army ended thus: "You are about to "take the oath of allegiance and obedience; and on my "part I solemnly vow always to be mindful of the fact "that the eyes of my ancestors are looking down upon "me from the other world, and that one day I shall have "to render to them an account both of the glory and "the honour of the Army " (June 15, 1888).

The distrust aroused by this *début* of the young war-lord did not vanish wholly ten days later when he assured the Reichstag: "I am determined to keep peace with "everyone so far as it lies in my power." He added that he would not use for aggressive purposes the army, which had been strengthened by the Army Bill of Feb. 6, 1888. Before long, the Kaiser's policy became more and more expansive, and his utterances more and more threatening. Here are some of them: "Our future lies upon the water"; "I will never rest until I have raised my Navy to a "position similar to that occupied by my Army"; "Ger-"man colonial aims can only be gained when Germany "has become master on the ocean."

The imprudence of these remarks is almost Bernhardi-like. Or rather, we may put it thus: that both the Emperor and Bernhardi have carried to excess the rule

of frank speech long practised with success by Bismarck
on the mendacious diplomatic circles of Frankfurt and
Vienna. The British people would not have paid much
attention to these utterances but for two important
considerations. Already, by the year 1888, Germany
had a large colonial Empire, sufficient for her present
needs and her administrative energies. Why, then,
should the young Kaiser proclaim his land-hunger, still
more, his devouring thirst? Again, if he intended to make
both his army and his navy supreme, such a policy
implied the adoption of plans dangerous to France,
Russia, and Great Britain. Would these Powers allow
such a policy to be pushed on to its natural conclusion?
For that conclusion was nothing less than supremacy
over the rest of the world. Thenceforth attention was
rivetted on the actions of William II. Would he, as he
often professed, aim at a peaceful ascendancy, in the
realms of science, manufacture and commerce? Or
would that mercantile power be only the spring-board from
which Germany would leap to world-supremacy in the
sphere of arms? That has been the question of questions
from 1890 to 1914.

The personality of a great man is the more interesting
because it can rarely be fathomed, or because its impulses
result from the clash of opposites, the triumph of which
can never be accurately gauged. On several occasions the
Kaiser has acted as a friend of peace. That fact must
never be forgotten. But whether it resulted from a
fixed resolve, or from the temporary restraint of prudential motives, can at present only be conjectured.
We do not know whether this war had its origin in his
fixed convictions and resolves; or, on the other hand,

whether his earlier peaceful tendencies were overborne
by external pressure at Court. There is a third alternative—that his own impatience at an admittedly trying
situation led him to force a way out at a time which he
deemed exceptionally favourable.

These alternatives we shall consider later. Meanwhile, we have seen that the Kaiser is a man of stimulating
personality and tremendous energy. He has energised
the German people to a degree never before known in
their history. Never before have they undergone sacrifices of man and treasure so appalling; and it is certain
that they have made those sacrifices, in part, for the
Kaiser, who to them embodies the Fatherland.

In this power of calling forth devotion, as also in the
riddle of his personality, he may challenge comparison
with Napoleon I. True, he is a smaller man at nearly
every point, except in regard to music and the arts. He
is not so successful an organiser, so acute a legislator, so
profound a strategist, as the Corsican. But in several
respects he resembles him. In both men we notice a
union of imaginative faculties and practical gifts. They
could dream dreams of a world-wide Empire and also
do much to prepare for their realization. To William as
to Napoleon there came the call of the Ocean; and both
felt the glamour of the Orient. Egypt, India, and parts
of America exercized a fascination on them; and alliances
and fleets, science and engineering, were pressed into their
service with feverish haste in order to be able to face the
Island Power which stood in their way. The vastness
of the resources at their command exercized a baneful
influence upon minds which were equally despotic and
unbending; while the neurotic strain in their natures led

them to insist on immediate and unquestioning obedience
both in trifling matters and in questions of high policy.
With Napoleon's sudden insistance that his architect
should on the very next day begin the construction of
the Carrousel Arch, of which as yet there was no plan,
compare the following account of William's fussy precipitation in regard to the conduct of foreign affairs
(1890):

> The Emperor wants to settle every detail, orders the Secretary
> of State, who has spent half the night at his desk, to submit the
> latest telegrams and advices to him in the very early morning, and
> then directs at once how everything must be arranged. Such a
> system leaves no room for the quiet consideration which should
> precede every decision. It is another bad feature that His Majesty
> so often deals privately with envoys[1].

The mania for control, natural to proud and restless
natures, told adversely both on the Corsican and the
Hohenzollern. The wider the domain over which it
ranges, the more imperious becomes the craving for
command, until what began with nervous interference
in details ends in megalomania fatal to a mighty Empire;
for, while the mind of the ruler revolves enterprises on
an ever vaster scale, his pedantic interferences reduce
counsellors to the level of clerks, thenceforth unable to
moderate the impulses of a diffuse and unbridled ambition.

Such a character, moreover, tends to excite and madden
a whole people; for men are thrilled not less by great
enterprises than by the alluring genius which appeals for
their accomplishment. Both Napoleon I and William II
had the power of firing all about them with their own
feverish energy and of interpreting the half-conscious

[1] M. Harden, p. 114.

desires of the multitude. Each leader professed at times
to work for peace; yet each led his nation to the brink
of disaster without foreseeing the dangers ahead. In
truth, both of them possessed greater energy than foresight, greater driving power than steering power. They
were good engineers but poor pilots. Now and again they
were obsessed by fits of passion that aroused fear and
distrust; so that we may apply to the Kaiser the sage
remark of Talleyrand about Napoleon: "He has never
"had but one dangerous conspirator against him—
"himself[1]."

If we test these men by comparing their position in
the periods of their rise and of their decline, we shall
find suggestive analogies. By their thirtieth year they
ruled as unquestioned masters over the greatest military
States in the world; and their neighbours looked to see
whether they would rest contented. As is well known,
the Peace of Amiens was, on the part of British Ministers,
an experiment. They wished to see whether the First
Consul would not be satisfied with the natural frontiers
and the development of the great France which his
genius had called to being. Similarly, the world has been
waiting to see whether the magnificent patrimony of the
German Empire and its many colonies would suffice for
William II; or whether he would challenge other States
of wide-spreading lands, notably the British and Russian
Empires and the vast domains of France.

There was much to give him pause. The career of
Napoleon, ending in ruin when he challenged both Russia
and Great Britain at the same time, should have prescribed caution. But, just as Napoleon in 1812 hacked

---

[1] *Mém. de Talleyrand*, II. p. 135.

his way through to Moscow, though he had of late been studying the disastrous Russian Campaign of Charles XII of Sweden, so, too, it would seem, Kaiser William has in him that overweening pride, that perverse obstinacy, which brooks no advice and scorns all difficulties, even if he has to bridge chasms with the corpses of his devoted followers. He, too, has challenged Russia and Great Britain at one and the same time, despite the warnings of his grandfather never to break with Russia, despite the advice of Bismarck not to offend needlessly the Island Power. Probably the Kaiser did not see whither his vague and grandiose schemes were leading him; for he comes of a family which prospered of late not so much by innate genius as by the genius of its counsellors. But surely ordinary prudence should have warned him that he was courting defeat in all quarters, at Paris and Petrograd, at London and Tokio.

His mistakes, or those of his Ministers, are more astounding than those of Napoleon. For the disaster of 1814 ought to have flashed a danger-signal, warning the Imperial watchman of 1914. But now and again there arise rulers on whom experience is thrown away. In them self-will is a disease; and their social charms serve but to spread broadcast the contagion of their warlike enthusiasm. From them and their paladins half a Continent catches the fatal frenzy; and, under the plea of national honour or national necessity, rushes to its doom.

LECTURE III

GERMANY'S WORLD-POLICY

"Das Schicksal Deutschlands ist, also, England."
(ROHRBACH, " Der deutsche Gedanke in der Welt." Preface.)

THE tremendous energy recently put forth by the
German people may be ascribed to various causes. The
Kaiser has during many years exerted upon them a
uniquely stimulating force, which has raised to blood heat
the political temperature of that people, the result being
that human energies of all kinds are pressed into the
service of the State to a degree which elsewhere is unknown.
Consequently, the nation is a fighting organism of un-
equalled efficiency, which, almost single-handed, has held
at bay three Great Powers.

This outburst of national energy is also due to the
German Universities. During many years there has
prevailed in those bodies an intensely patriotic feeling,
which may be traced largely to the teachings of Treitschke.
Saxon though he was, he, somewhat like young Körner
before him, became an enthusiastic Prussian; and his
lectures on History at Berlin (1874–1896) helped on the
growth of the new German Chauvinism. He idolized
Prussia because she embodied the ideal of power. Apart

from her, Germany was backboneless. With her, Germany
could become, nay, must become, a World Power. Strength
was the supreme political virtue. Weakness the supreme
political vice. In Bk I. of *Die Politik* he defines the
State as—"the public power of offence and defence."
He dismisses at once Hegel's notion of the State as the
totality of the people. According to Treitschke, the
State is something over and above the people: "The
"State protects and embraces the life of the people,
"regulating it externally in all directions....It demands
"obedience: its laws must be kept, whether willingly or
"unwillingly....The State says: 'It is quite indifferent
" 'to me what you think about the matter, but you must
" 'obey.' " And again: "The renunciation of its own
"power is for the State in the most real sense the sin
"against the Holy Ghost."

Treitschke asserted emphatically that Germany ought
to expand. The triumph of 1870 must not satisfy her.
All great States, he says, will continue to develop by an
inflexible law of Nature: "He is a fool who believes that
"this process of development can ever cease."

At whose expense must Germany expand? Treitschke
left it in no doubt. A new world, that of the non-European
peoples, is coming within the scope of our activities; and
the European States must subdue them, directly or
indirectly. England was first in the race for World-
Empire; and by force or fraud she seized the best lands:
"England, while posing as the defender of Liberalism,
"egged on the European States against one another,
"kept Europe in a condition of latent unrest, and mean-
"while conquered half the world. And if she continues
"to be successful in maintaining this condition of unrest

"on the Continent, she will put many more countries
"into her big pocket."

Treitschke, it will be seen, furbishes up the romances
of the pre-scientific chroniclers, who tried to prove that
Louis XIV and XV, even the Great Napoleon himself,
were the *agents provocateurs* of England. The insatiable
islanders set the world in a turmoil in order to colour red
new lands beyond the seas. Treitschke and his many
followers, if they were logical, would affirm that Germany's
annexation of Alsace-Lorraine was due to perfidious
Albion, because it kept Germany and France at enmity.
The Eastern Question would also prove to be a happy
hunting-ground for mares' nests of the same general
description.

Nevertheless, his work claims careful attention. For
he pointed the Germans towards a World-Empire. He
also urged them to develop political strength in order to
found that Empire on the ruins of that of Great Britain.
Some German professors, notably Paulsen, have combatted
his teaching, but with little success. The spirit of
Treitschke has for some few years past dominated the
German Universities, and through them the schools of
that land. Therefore young Germans have grown up to
believe that they must one day fight Great Britain.

Further, the population question pushes Germany
on. For the most part it is inland peoples that have
most severely felt the pressure of a growing population.
Islanders and coast-dwellers can expand over the seas. But
when inland peoples outgrow their bounds, they must burst
them. Tacitus in his *Germania* noted this tendency among
the Teutons of his day, and observed that their young
champions frequently swarmed off from the parent hive.

In olden times, as today, the fertility of that people has been very marked. Consequently, it has become scattered, and political unity has been more and more difficult to attain. These are the dominating facts of German life. The population-problem often recurs; and yet it is with difficulty solved because the nation has with difficulty acted as a whole.

After the war of 1870 Germany attained political union; but, even so, she could not escape the cramping conditions of her life. Nay, they fettered her more and more, as her prosperity increased. Note the following figures of her population:

1871	..	..	41,000,000
1890	..	..	49,400,000
1900	..	..	56,400,000
1913	..	..	66,000,000 (?)

Only one European people increases faster, viz. the Russian; and the Russians can overflow into Siberia. In earlier times our population-problem was serious; but our people migrated to new lands across the seas, which could be had almost for the asking. Germany, pressed by the same problem, has had to put up with the less desirable lands. Is it surprising that she feels land-hunger? Endowed with a keen sense of national pride, she was certain to experience some such feeling; and we, who have expanded partly by force of arms, partly by a natural overflow of population, shall be foolishly blind if we do not try to understand the enemy's point of view. The militant German of today is consciously or unconsciously harking back to the primitive times when the young Teutonic bloods persuaded the tribal meeting to let them lead forth a band of warriors to a land of plenty. The mythical Hengists and Horsas, with their longboats girt about with shields, foreshadowed Kaiser Wilhelm sending forth his legions, his warships, his submarines, his Zeppelins. The events of today are a hideous recurrence to the primeval state. Viewed in regard to its innermost causes, the present war is an attempt at a *Volkswanderung*; and the atrocities that mark its course may perhaps be ascribed, in part at least, to a superabundant national energy, which, finding itself cramped, forces its way out on the line of least resistance towards the coveted maritime outlets, Salonica on the South East, Antwerp and Ostend on the North West. The longing for World-Policy (*Weltpolitik*) is merely a modern expression of an old Teutonic instinct.

In this sense, our war with Germany is one of people against people. The fact must be faced. It has been asserted that the war was due to the Kaiser or to a few wicked persons at Berlin. That is incorrect. At least, it is only half the explanation. At bottom, the war is a determined and desperate effort of the German people to force its way through to more favourable political conditions. They refuse to see the great majority of their emigrants for ever lost to the Fatherland. They are resolved at all costs to conquer some large part or parts of the world where German colonists can live and bring up families under the black-white-and-red flag. They have definitely rejected the Free Trade ideal, which looks on the world as potentially a single economic unit. They have adopted with ardour the narrowly national ideals set forth by the Kaiser and Treitschke. They laugh at Free Trade theories as good only for college lecture-rooms. They also reject the notion of economic spheres of influence, which might possibly have satisfied them if they had not become obsessed by the new gospel of power. But they are obsessed by it; and they intend to become the great World-Power.

Early in the reign of the present Kaiser it was clear that German policy would take a far wider and higher flight. The policy of Bismarck was deemed antiquated. The old Chancellor had sought by a careful system of alliances to secure the position of Germany in Europe. He succeeded. He built up the Triple Alliance; and France and Great Britain and Russia were politically isolated. He had secured many colonies; but not enough for the young Kaiser. The colonial movement was to be accelerated and form part of a system of World-Policy[1]. The quarrel between the Kaiser and Bismarck in 1890 must have arisen owing to some question of more than personal import; for the latter at once ordered his secretary, Busch, to sort his papers and send them away for fear that the Kaiser might seize them. He also said that spies had been set to watch him[2].

The Kaiser did not plunge heedlessly into the new policy; for, indeed, in conduct he is generally more prudent than in speech. In 1890 he framed an agreement with Great Britain whereby Germany definitely secured

[1] The Germans are generally unfair to Bismarck, forgetting that most of their colonies were acquired by him. Thus, Prince von Bülow says (*Imperial Germany*, Eng. edit. pp. 9, 10): "It is certain that "Bismarck did not foresee the course of this new development of "Germany." And again: "If the course of events demands that we "transcend the limits of Bismarck's aims, then we must do so."

[2] *Bismarck; Some Secret Pages*, III. 309; M. Harden, *Monarchs and Men*, ch. III. The general explanation is that the Kaiser disliked Bismarck's anti-socialist measures.

possession of the large domains now known as German East Africa and German South-West Africa. On the other hand, we acquired Nyassaland and Somaliland, which, in reality, ought not to have been in dispute. And, in order to clinch this not very satisfactory bargain, we surrendered to Germany the long coveted island, Heligoland. It is well to recall the terms in which Count Münster first proposed the transfer of Heligoland to Germany in the year 1884. He assured our Foreign Minister, Lord Granville, that the transfer of Heligoland would be deemed a most friendly act, and he skilfully represented it as furthering the cause of peace (see Lecture I.). As at that time the colonial rivalry of the two lands was very keen, the British Government waved aside the proposal. But the Kaiser in 1890 renewed his offers; and they were favourably received at London, because Lord Salisbury's Government wished to clear up all outstanding disputes. Now, we may admit that it was an extremely important matter to arrange the "partition of Africa" without a war. Considering the rivers of blood that have flowed for the possession, say, of the Spice Islands in the East Indies, and Cuba and Hayti in the West Indies, it was a triumph of the cause of peace to arrange a friendly partition of the centre and south of a mighty Continent. The previous decade had bristled with contentious questions; and it was well to get three-fourths of them settled in a friendly manner, as we endeavoured to do.

Then, again, Heligoland was worth far more to Germany than it was to us; and in such a case the amicable course was to barter it away in return for concessions by Germany. Further, the island could have been fortified

4—2

only at enormous cost, which an eminent authority has placed at £2,000,000; and it was quite certain that Parliament would have refused any such sum for an islet which was then deemed certain to disappear beneath the waves.

At the same time, it must be admitted that the transfer was a serious blunder; for it brought within the range of possibility the vast maritime schemes of the Kaiser. Thereafter, he pushed on the Kiel Canal; and it is significant that the opening ceremony, on June 18, 1895, became what a German writer has termed "a magnificent demonstration in favour of peace." The Kaiser himself described the canal as "this new link for the blessing "and peace of the nations." But, as he also referred to the squadrons of ironclads of various Powers there present as "a symbol of peace," the exact nature of the mission to be fulfilled by the canal remained matter for doubt.

The year 1895 witnessed a notable extension of the activities of Germany. She opposed strenuously the British proposals respecting the Congo Free State, which was then becoming a standing disgrace to civilization; and sharp friction ensued in the Press on this question.

Far more important was the Kaiser's action in the Far East. Early in the year 1895 China was hopelessly beaten by Japan; and the victorious islanders prepared to retain their chief conquest, viz., the Liao-tung Peninsula, with its commanding fortress, Port Arthur. Russia, backed up by both France and Germany, vigorously opposed this acquisition; and the *Kölnische Zeitung* in an evidently inspired article, declared that Japan was obviously bent on encircling China and cutting her off from commerce with the outer world. The three Powers on April 23 demanded that Japan should withdraw from Port Arthur and the whole of the Peninsula; and Japan, exhausted by the war, had to give up the chief fruits of her triumph. Ever since, she has remembered that Great Britain took no share in that act of coercion. But she has remembered the part then played by Germany; and in August 1914 she tasted the sweets of an ironical revenge. In her ultimatum to Germany, bidding her hand back the Shantung Peninsula to China, she made use of the same haughty terms employed by Germany towards her in 1895.

In the year 1897 Germany took a notable step forward in World-Policy by the seizure of Kiao-Chao. That act was due to the Kaiser himself. It was carried through against the protests of the German Chancellor, Prince Hohenlohe, and was therefore a breach of the German constitution[1]. As is well known, the murder of two German missionaries furnished the pretext for that high-handed action. However, Mr Skertchley, a mining prospector, has stated that he had recently published a metallurgical map of that peninsula which showed it to be rich in minerals. We may therefore conjecture that the motive of the Germans was subterranean rather than celestial.

At that time the break up of the Chinese Empire seemed imminent, and England in 1898 secured Wei-hei-wei as a counterpart to Germany's late acquisition. The would-be partitioning Powers were disappointed; for China displayed an obstinate vitality. After the Boxer Rising, Great Britain did much to check all schemes of the Western Powers by concluding the very important

[1] W. von Schierbrand, p. 31.

agreement of January 30, 1902, with Japan. Not only did
it proclaim the entry of Japan into the circle of the Great
Powers, but it served to check the inroads of the white
race upon the yellow race which the Kaiser and others
sought to justify by descanting upon "The Yellow
Peril." Thenceforth schemes of partition of China fell
into the background, and so did the Yellow Peril. When
the whole truth is known, it will probably be found
that the Anglo-Japanese alliance gave pause not only
to Russia but also to Germany. Her World-Policy, so
far as concerned the Far East, must have aimed at
prizes far vaster than Kiao-Chao; but, as things have
turned out, it began with Kiao-Chao, and it ended with
Kiao-Chao.

Herr Rohrbach, one of the exponents of German
World-Policy, especially in the Levant, has observed
that that ideal is characterized by vagueness, and that
with difficulty it concentrates on any one aim[1]. Its
diffuseness will be apparent in this lecture and the following. Indeed, this must be my excuse for making here
an abrupt transition from China to South Brazil. The
latter country has long attracted the attention of the
German colonial party. Its climate, though sub-tropical,
is not unhealthy; the material resources are immense;
and during many years there has been a large influx
of German immigrants. Their numbers have been
variously estimated from a million to as low as 350,000.
The German immigration does not equal the Italian.
But the Teuton scorns both the native Portuguese
element and the Italians, still more the half-castes. He
is conscious of superior vigour; and he feels the power

[1] P. Rohrbach, *Deutschland unter den Weltvölkern*, p. 55.

of the Fatherland behind him. The German settlements in Brazil are compact: their schools are supported from home; 10,000 German school-books have of late been sent out; and the teaching of Portuguese is forbidden. The poverty of the Brazilian exchequer has long warranted the hope that the country would come under German control. But American opinion, grounded upon the Monroe Doctrine, defies Germany to interfere in any part of South America; and there is in the States a wide-spread conviction that, if the Kaiser succeeds in this war, he will next attack them.

It is difficult for a Briton to form an unbiassed judgment on the Brazilian Question; but of all Germany's colonial aims (and they are surprisingly wide and diffuse) those which centre in Southern Brazil seem the most reasonable. The land is enormous; the inhabitants are inferior to those whom Germany sends out; and a German Southern Brazil would add to the productivity of the world and to the welfare of mankind. But to this scheme the United States oppose an invincible opposition. Probably they are right; for, with the spectacle of European armaments before them, they naturally dread the incoming of German militarism into the New World, the southern part of which, including Argentina, would in that case fall to the Teuton.

In April, 1897, the journal, *Die Grenzboten*, naïvely stated—" The possession of South Africa offers greater " advantages in every respect than that of Brazil." The assertion may serve to remind us of the clash of German and British interests in that land from 1895 to the present year. There was much to recommend South Africa to the Germans. Possessing a splendid climate, in which the white race attains to physical perfection, holding the keys of the Indian and Southern Oceans, peopled, also, mainly by Dutch, and dowered by Nature with the richest stores of gold and diamonds in the world, South Africa was for the Pan-Germans the new Deutschland of the South, a home for myriads of Teutons, a source of endless wealth, the key to the Orient. The dealings of Germany with the South African Republic and the Orange Free State are, of course, not fully known. We therefore must fall back on the British Blue Books, which, however, are at points very suggestive.

In the year 1895 the condition of South Africa was alarming. The discontent of the Outlanders in the South African Republic (Transvaal) was on the increase. Debarred from all political rights, though their energy and wealth filled the once empty Exchequer, they demanded the franchise and other reforms which would render their position bearable. As is well known, President Krüger resisted their demands. He also openly proclaimed his reliance on Kaiser William. At an official banquet given at Pretoria on the Kaiser's birthday (January 27, 1895) he said, "I shall ever promote "the interests of Germany.... The time has come to "knit ties of the closest friendship between Germany "and the South African Republic—ties such as are "natural between father and child[1]."

These ties were very profitable to both parties. Germans and Hollanders acquired the dynamite monopoly, the spirit monopoly, and many others, of course for large sums of money; and the Berlin Government showed

---

[1] Fitzpatrick, *The Transvaal from Within*, p. 106; Reventlow, *Deutschlands auswärtige Politik*, pp. 69, 70.

its gratitude by sending to Krüger decorations galore, until his quaint farmer-figure was a very Christmas-tree of geegaws. In the autumn of 1895 his right-hand man, Dr Leyds, visited Lisbon and Berlin; and he is known to have ordered quantities of arms in Germany. Everything seemed to portend a German Protectorate over the Transvaal. The Germans and Dutch supported Krüger against the Reform party, which was therefore driven to desperation. On December 24, 1895, the German Consul notified to the Kaiser that the Outlanders and their British supporters were hatching a plot to overthrow the Government. On the 30th the German residents begged the Kaiser to protect them; and on that day the Consul asked permission to order up from Delagoa Bay a detachment of German sailors and marines from the warship, *Seeadler*. They would have been sent if the crisis had not passed by very quickly, before the Portuguese Government gave permission for their des-patch through its territory[1]. When Dr Jameson's Raid ended in utter failure, the Kaiser promptly sent a telegram of congratulation to Krüger (January 3, 1896). This act was unfriendly to us; but far more unfriendly was the re-solve to send German sailors and marines up to Pretoria. In case Dr Jameson's Raid had succeeded, we should soon have been face to face with a German contingent at that capital. This, perhaps, explains the phrase in the Kaiser's telegram to Krüger, congratulating him, " that you and your people have succeeded by your own energy, without appealing to the aid of friendly Powers, in defeating the armed forces," etc. If we look at the telegram in the light of this fact, it is less provocative

[1] F. Rachfahl, *Kaiser und Reich* (1888–1913), Berlin, 1913, p. 144.

than appears on the surface. Indeed, the Kaiser's words probably express a sense of relief that war would not ensue between Great Britain and Germany[1]. Further, when the British Press broke forth into unmeasured protests against the Kaiser's interference in matters which did not concern him, the German Government declared that they were concerned about their important commercial interests in the Transvaal, and that no offence was meant by the Emperor's telegram at the defeat of " a lawless armed band," organized by the Chartered Company. Technically, we were in the wrong; and Mr Chamberlain promptly disavowed the raiders.

On the whole, it seems unlikely that the Kaiser then desired war, though he would have accepted war if his forces and ours collided at Pretoria, as would have happened if the Jameson Raid had succeeded. It must be remembered that the German fleet was not in a condition to face the British fleet; and further, the relations between Paris and Berlin were somewhat strained since the month of November 1895, when the Radical Ministry of M. Bourgeois came to power. It was an energetic Ministry. " We demand your confidence, not to exist, " but to act "—such were his first words to the Chamber of Deputies. He also assured Great Britain that France had only one enemy, of course, Germany[2]. Thus, at the time of the Jameson Raid the policy of Berlin was dominated by two considerations, weakness at sea, and the renewed hostility of the French, who by then felt sure of the support of Russia. At that period, apparently,

---

[1] I came to this conclusion before reading the arguments of Reventlow, pp. 73–5.

[2] Rachfahl, p. 145.

Germany and Austria (for Italy was of little account after her colonial disasters) did not feel equal to a war with Great Britain, France and Russia, a combination which was then within the bounds of probability. But, undoubtedly, the friction between Britons and Germans first became acute at the time of the Jameson Raid. Crispi in his *Memoirs* states that, previous to that event, Kaiser William referred jocularly to a passing tiff with England, " Bah! it's a lovers' quarrel[1]." But Count Reventlow significantly asserts that the crisis of 1895–6 would not have ended as it did if Germany had been strong at sea[2]. She felt her weakness; and in the year 1897 the Kaiser took steps which portended a great advance. He appointed Count (afterwards Prince) Bülow Secretary of Foreign Affairs, and Admiral von Tirpitz, a man of great energy, Secretary of the Admiralty. Both men were actuated by anti-British feelings, though Bülow naïvely confesses that it was needful to conceal them until the new fleet was ready. In 1898, then, came the first German Navy Law providing for a great increase in warships of all classes; but, to his annoyance, the new fleet was not ready by the time of the Boer War[3].

Before that struggle curious events happened at Johannesburg, notably the so-called British plot of May, 1899. It was probably trumped up by the Krüger Government. Three of the alleged conspirators were *agents provocateurs* of that administration. A man named Bundy, one of the more reputable of the persons arrested, was privately

[1] Crispi, *Mems.* III. p. 328 (Eng. edit.), " Bah! was sich liebt, neckt sich."

[2] Reventlow, p. 96.

[3] Bülow, *Imperial Germany*, pp. 19–31 (Eng. edit.).

told, after the first examination, that his evidence was
very unsatisfactory because it did not implicate the
Reformers; and Krüger's son, chief of the Secret Service,
said to him in private, "Do all you can to prove this
"to be a case of conspiracy on the part of the British
"Government, as it will strengthen my father's hand....
"I will give you £200, and you shall get a good billet
"in the Secret Service." The Transvaal Government
thereupon telegraphed both to Paris and Berlin its
version of the trial.

Now, all this happened just before the Bloemfontein
Conference, from which the British Government expected
a peaceful and satisfactory settlement of the Transvaal
Question. It is clear, then, that Krüger placed great
hopes in Germany; and he was bitterly disappointed
during the war, when that Government did not accord
the armed support for which its people clamoured. He
proceeded to Germany, in the hope, doubtless, of forcing
the Kaiser's hand; but the Kaiser, alleging a previous
hunting engagement, declined to receive him. Rarely
has the German Press been so outspoken against their
sovereign; and its protests were renewed when, after
the war, Generals Botha, Delarey and De Wet also met
with no official countenance. The Pan-Germans lauded
the Generals to the skies; and their Press dubbed Botha
the organizer of victory; Delarey the actual victor; and
De Wet the Blücher of South Africa. The attitude of
the official world at Berlin was, however, quite correct;
and the moral of the situation was pointed by a leader
of the German National Liberals. He asked what was
the use of all this fuss? Why did not Germans leave
Great Britain alone until their navy was stronger? Also

the *Kölnische Zeitung*, an official organ, even went so far as naïvely to ask—Why had the Boer Generals come to Germany, of all countries, in order to stir up trouble? The events of October, 1914, supply the answer.

The Boer War roused to fury the anti-British feeling already strong in Germany; or, as Professor Mommsen mildly phrased it, "The war accentuated the antagonism, "but did not produce it." Very noteworthy, too, was the influence of the struggle on the agitation for a larger Navy. The sense of irritation at the inability of Germany to cope with the British fleet was skilfully exploited both by the Kaiser and by the German Navy League. In 1900, during that conflict, the naval programme of 1898 was accelerated. Many branches of the Navy League were founded; and every new foundation, every launch of a battleship, evoked a stirring speech from the Kaiser. These orations were not, as a rule, threatening to Great Britain; but now and again came a sentence, such as "The trident must pass into our hands." The meaning was clear enough. Kaiser William was bent on forcing into a practical channel the foaming flood of Anglo-phobia; and in this he showed statesmanship of a high order. Had he been merely the garrulous and impression-able creature of our comic papers, he would have let the Germans froth and foam. Instead of that, he built a larger navy.

These events did not escape the keen eyes of His late Majesty, Edward VII. He knew full well the perils of those years. He must have discerned the danger ahead if the Boer War were prolonged. The Pan-Germans strove might and main to lengthen out that war. The *Deutsche Zeitung* went so far as to say, "Every work

" of civilization [in South Africa] built with English
" money must be destroyed. The land must be devastated
" in such a way that only the Boer farmer can live in it."
The aim of all that devastation was, so far as we can
judge, to prolong the Boer War until the year 1904
when the new German navy would be ready. But that
unhappy struggle ended in 1902, partly owing to the
success of the British arms, partly owing to the generous
terms offered by the victors. The policy of conciliation
had the approval of King Edward; conciliation towards
the Boers helped both to end that war and thereafter to
weld South Africa into an almost united whole.

Further, we probably owe to him the friendly under-
standings with other Powers which ended the period
of what was pompously termed " splendid isolation."
The danger of that makeshift policy having been sufficiently obvious during the Boer War, it was desirable
to come to an understanding with some Power or Powers.

With whom should it be? With Germany? That
was a possibility. On dynastic and racial grounds there
was much to recommend an Anglo-German alliance. Or
should it be with our old enemy, France? King Edward
clearly believed that an Anglo-French *Entente* was more
feasible. Whatever the motives that prompted the
choice, King Edward advocated a *rapprochement* towards
France; and, as is well known, he did very much to
further it. The reasons for not making the experiment
at Berlin doubtless were that the Kaiser displayed
increasing eagerness in regard to World-Policy; and
parliamentary considerations led him throughout the
years 1895–1904 to rely more and more upon the agrarian
party, the party of the Junkers, which was furiously

anti-British. The questions directly at issue between the two countries were less serious than those which divided England from France; but the trend of German politics rendered it more difficult to come to an understanding with our Teutonic kinsmen than with our affable and democratic neighbours across the Channel. Efforts were made both in the British and German Press to cultivate friendlier relations; but they failed, and largely owing to the growth in Germany of the Pan-German movement. To this we must now advert.

The Pan-Germans aim at some form of union of all peoples speaking German or certain of its dialects. It is not a new notion. Generations of students had enthusiastically intoned the famous line at the end of Arndt's national song of 1813,

Das ganze Deutschland soll es sein.

And for a brief space in 1848–9 it seemed that a greater Germany might come to being. The miscarriage of democratic Imperialism in that land is one of the greatest misfortunes of the Nineteenth Century; for the federation then contemplated would have harmonized the claims of national unity with those of the sovereignty of the people. Further, the German race, when fitly organized, could then have shared in the new lands beyond the seas which were then easily obtainable. In that case the British Empire might not have been quite so large; but probably we should not have had this war, which, on its colonial side, is the deliberate attempt of the Kaiser and his people to seize lands appropriated by earlier competitors in the race for Empire. As Bernhardi says: " All which other nations attained in cen-
" turies of natural development—political union, colonial

" possessions, naval power, international trade—was de-
" nied to our nation until quite recently[1]."

The grievance was a real one; and therein lay the
strength of the Pan-German movement. The clubs which
adopted the colours of the old Empire—black, red,
gold—sought to band together all their kindred in some
kind of organism. The first sentence of the manifesto
is as follows: "The Pan-German Federation has for
" object the revival of German national sentiment all
" over the earth: the preservation of German thought,
" ideals and customs in Europe and across the ocean,
" and the welding into a compact whole of Germans
" everywhere." Obviously, the crux of the whole question
lies in the last clause; for nobody could possibly object
to the preservation of German thought and ideals. But
what is meant by " the welding into a compact whole
" of the Germans everywhere"? It must mean the
inclusion in a Greater Germany of the 12,000,000 Germans
in the Austrian Empire, and the million or so of Germans
in the Baltic Provinces of Russia. But does it include
the Dutch, the Flemings, and the Scandinavian peoples?
Many enthusiastic Teutons assert that all those peoples
are branches of the great stock. Thus, the geographical
manual of Herr Daniel declares that the natural limits
of Germany are the River Narova, in Esthonia, on the
North-East, the Baltic on the North, the North Sea on
the North-West, on the West the hills separating the
Rhine and Seine basins, and on the South and South-East
the Bernese Alps and the Carpathians. Up to the month
of August, 1914, there were a few prominent citizens
of Antwerp who desired to see the fulfilment of the Pan-

---

[1] Bernhardi, *The Next War*, ch. 4.

German scheme of making that city the chief Teutonic port.

The Pan-German movement suffers from the defect which has always clogged the German polity, namely, indefiniteness. No definition of Pan-Germanism has appeared which brought it within the region of practical politics, except as the result of a terrific war. For the German people is not a compact entity. It spreads, octopus-like, from the Alpine, Tyrolese, and Styrian valleys to the mouth of the River Ems, and from the banks of the middle Moselle to the Gulf of Finland. Therefore, the welding of these outlying portions into the main body implies the break-up of the Austrian Empire, the annexation of Luxemburg and nearly half of Switzerland, as well as the acquisition of the best part of Russia's all too scanty seaboard. With the exception, perhaps, of the Swiss part of the menu, which might come as dessert after the main repast, all these questions are, or may be, at stake in the present war. An All-German Empire would involve as terrible a political upheaval as the formation of a Pan-Slav Empire to which it is a Teutonic retort.

But there is even more than this behind the Pan-German Movement. For practical purposes it has adopted the programme of *Weltpolitik*. This again suffered from the defect of haziness. So far as I know, the Kaiser, who coined the phrase, has never defined it. He took refuge in vague statements like this (July 3, 1900), " The wave-beat knocks powerfully at our gates " and calls us as a great nation to maintain our place " in our world—in other words, to pursue world-policy. " The ocean is indispensable for Germany's greatness; " but the ocean also reminds us that neither on it nor

" across it in the distance can any great decision be again
" arrived at without Germany and the German Emperor."

He uttered these words during the Boer War. They
are open to two explanations. Either the Kaiser may
not have meant as much as he said; that is, in Disraeli's
historic phrase, " he was carried away by the exuberance
" of his own verbosity." Or else he meant that Germany
was going to interfere in every great occurrence all over
the world. And those who noted the Kaiser's skill
as a speaker and his feverish activities were bound to
take this explanation. Of the same order were these
utterances: " The trident must pass into our hands ";
and " Our future lies upon the water." They can be
interpreted only as a definite and defiant challenge to
Great Britain; and in earlier and more heedless times
they would have led straight to war. Fortunately, the
Islanders did not lose their temper, but merely redoubled
their precautions. So did Russia; so did France; so
did the United States; so did Japan. A single pronouncement of that kind might be discounted as due to a desire
to expedite a New Navy Bill. But those dicta, when
repeated, could not be thus explained. From Washington
to Paris; from London to Tokio the question arose, "Where
" will the mailed fist fall next? "

During several years the Pan-German movement
aroused much ridicule; and Britons especially refused
to take it seriously. We were wrong. These notions,
which seem to us fantastic and unstatesmanlike, made
a deep impression in Germany and German Austria.
They touched the romantic strain, which is strong in the
Teuton, and also appealed to his sense of national pride,
which had been enormously inflated by the uninterrupted

triumphs of the years 1864–1871. The Pan-German ideal supplied the young nation with two requisites for action—a theory attractive to superficial thinkers and a fighting creed for the masses. It became the dominant ideal of the German race; and those who held to the cautious nationalism of Bismarck were deemed fossilized survivals of an age which would soon be eclipsed by triumphs greater than Sedan.

We must therefore dismiss from our minds the thought that we are at war merely with a Government which has blinded its subjects. That is inconsistent with the facts of the situation. It is also not a struggle with a dominant military caste, which may be overthrown after a few defeats. We are at war with a practically united nation. The energy with which wave after wave of old men and boys of the German reserve or Landsturm swept on to almost certain overthrow near Ypres ought to open our eyes to the fact that we are facing a nation in arms, a nation which is resolved at all costs to conquer. For the prize of triumph is a World-Empire; whereas defeat will imply that their population-problem will be solved by the most horrible of all methods, depopulation.

LECTURE IV

MOROCCO: THE BAGDAD RAILWAY

In the previous lecture it was apparent that many
strands went to make up the imposing cable of Germany's
World-Policy. We then glanced at two of them—South
Africa and Brazil. But two others are equally important
—Morocco and the Bagdad Railway.

The European Powers have often endeavoured to
secure a footing in Morocco. Great Britain and Spain
were first in the field; and up to the year 1890 their
interests in Morocco were supreme. But after that time
France manifested designs of far-reaching scope. They
comprised all the land from Cape Bon to the Straits of
Gibraltar; from Tangier to the Gulf of Guinea. North-
West Africa was to form a solid block of French territory,
broken only by a few British enclaves at the Gambia and
the Lower Niger. With the conclusion of the Franco-
Russian alliance in 1894 and the end of the Algerian
rising in 1900, these vast plans gained in consistency;
and with the twentieth century Morocco became one of
the danger-points of the political horizon. At first the
chief friction was between Great Britain, France, and
Spain. Their interests outweighed those of Germany;
and at that time France looked upon us as her worst

competitor in commerce, while Spain clung jealously to the long cherished hope of conquest of the Moors. Her interests centred in Tangier and Tetuan; those of France in the North-East and East and centre; for, obviously, she could not allow anarchy to prevail among the Moors of the East, lest Algeria should once more revolt. The interests of Great Britain were, in the main, commercial; but we could not see unmoved the acquisition of the coast facing Gibraltar by a great maritime Power; and the critical points were Tangier, Ceuta, and possible coaling-stations on the Atlantic coast. For Germany the most desirable points were good harbours on the south part of the Atlantic coast of Morocco. The best were Mogador and Agadir, though the latter is a very indifferent port, which never could shelter large cruisers.

The aims of the four Powers were not hopelessly opposed; but the tension between them became keen early in the twentieth century. During the South African War France pushed ahead fast in Morocco, the propelling force at Paris being a very masterful personality. Delcassé represented the ardent national spirit of young France, the France which rejoiced in the Russian alliance and believed itself strong enough to carry the tricolour into new lands. True, the Fashoda experiment had failed, owing to the lack of the expected support from Russia. Throughout the year 1898 and during the Boer War the French Press was extremely bitter against us; but Delcassé remained unmoved by the storm of words. He, the political heir of Gambetta, saw in England a potential ally, in Germany the only enemy[1].

[1] R. Pinon, *France et Allemagne*, pp. 97–110; Reventlow, *Deutschlands auswärtige Politik*, pp. 126–8.

Foiled in the hope of pushing a belt of French influence
across the Soudan and even to the Red Sea, France
turned to Morocco. Her opportunity came during the
South African War; and in December 1900 she "squared"
Italy by agreeing that the Government of Rome should
have a free hand in Tripoli if that of Paris worked its will
in Morocco. This compact explains why Italy lent but
a feeble support to her ally, Germany, in the Moroccan
dispute.

Delcassé next approached the Court of Madrid. In
the years 1901–2 he sought to frame a secret bargain
whereby Spain should acquire North and North Central
Morocco and France the remainder. But Great Britain,
hearing of this clandestine "deal," managed to arouse
Spanish sentiment against an affair none too flattering
to the national pride. The Ministry resigned and its
successors broke off the affair. Delcassé then turned to
Great Britain, a Power which evidently must be satisfied
before the tricolour could wave at Fez. Now, there
were many topics in dispute between us and France.
We had not settled the West African boundary disputes,
or those relating to the Newfoundland fisheries, or to
Madagascar and the New Hebrides. Above all, France
had never forgiven us for occupying Egypt in 1882, though
she herself had then refused to share in the dangers and
burdens of the Egyptian enterprise. To settle all these
outstanding disputes seemed impossible. Yet, owing to
the tact of Edward VII, and the skill of Lord Lansdowne
and Delcassé, it was accomplished in April, 1904, by a
series of agreements which paved the way towards an
Anglo-French Entente. The chief points which concern
us here are these. France recognised our position in

Egypt, while we admitted that France had predominant claims and interests in Morocco, especially in assuring order. France declared that she would not alter the political status of that land; and we gave a similar promise about Egypt. But the first secret article attached to the Convention specified that both France and Great Britain might find themselves "constrained by force of "circumstances to modify this policy in respect to Egypt "or Morocco." By this questionable device both Governments left themselves a loophole for escaping from the public promise. In the third secret article the Spanish sphere of influence was roughly defined as the Mediterranean area of Morocco[1]. The Franco-Spanish agreement, foreshadowed by this secret article, came about in October, 1904, when Spain gained a reversionary claim to that area.

The outstanding fact in the Anglo-French Entente is that the Powers earnestly desired to end their differences. Where there was the will, a way was found. To Delcassé belongs the credit of terminating the feuds between the two lands arising out of the Fashoda affair and the Boer War; and to the Deputies, *e.g.* Deschanel, who reproached him with abandoning historic claims in Egypt, he retorted that the British occupation of the Nile valley was an accomplished fact, and that France would find Morocco of a hundred times greater value than Egypt, especially because the Moors would prove to be excellent troops for colonial service. We may note in passing that there had previously been proposals of an Anglo-German-Japanese

---

[1] E. D. Morel, *Morocco in Diplomacy*, ch. x; Tardieu, *Questions diplomatiques de* 1904, p. 313; R. Pinon, *France et Allemagne* (1870–1913), (Appendix), for documents.

entente, but it fell through, chiefly because Germany refused to take a course of action which might in the future tie her hands with regard to naval programmes and *Weltpolitik*[1]. She further preferred to approach Russia probably with a view to joint aggressive action in the Far East. The results of her encouragement to the Court of Petrograd will soon appear.

Meanwhile France, Great Britain, and Spain were gaining over Morocco the control of the purse. The Sultan of Morocco was extravagant and careless, therefore always in debt. The state of Moroccan finances was reflected in the prayer which is always affixed to any official reference to that Exchequer—"May God fill it." With oriental exuberance, the same prayer is added at any mention of the name of the Chancellor of the Exchequer: "May God keep him full[2]." The half only of the prayer was answered; for the Chancellor was always full, but his Exchequer was always empty.

France, Great Britain, and Spain undertook to play the part of a maleficent Providence. As might be expected, these dealings of France, Great Britain, and Spain with Morocco caused annoyance at Berlin. At first, it is true, that Government showed surprising calm respecting the Anglo-French agreement, and Count Bülow declared in the Reichstag on April 12, 1904, that, on the whole, Germany welcomed a good understanding between those two Powers as consolidating the peace of the world; that the chief question was as to Morocco, and German interests in that land were solely economic. This was reassuring enough; and the Franco-Spanish agreement

[1] Reventlow, pp. 229–235.
[2] Tardieu. *Questions diplomatiques de* 1904, p. 58.

also aroused no protest, probably because its secret articles were not then known[1]. But in the spring of the year 1905 there came a change which is highly significant; for it shows how completely German policy depended on outward circumstances. In a word it was *Realpolitik*.

A change in the Balance of Power had come about owing to two chief events. Germany had completed her naval programme, planned in 1898 and increased during the Boer War. And Russia, early in March, had sustained that terrible defeat at Mukden at the hands of the Japanese. For the present, then, Russia, and therefore the Franco-Russian Alliance, could be neglected. Germany at once saw her chance. On March 12 it was officially announced that Kaiser William, in the course of a Mediterranean cruise, would visit Tangiers, and the announcement was made in an emphatic manner. When Herr Bebel, the Socialist leader, twitted the Chancellor with the hard and almost threatening tone of his references to Morocco, he replied: "I must remind him that the "language and attitude of diplomatists and politicians is "regulated according to circumstances. The moment "that I judge favourable for the setting forth of German "interests, I choose it according to my own opinion." Two days later (March 31) the Kaiser suddenly landed at Tangiers, and declared that he visited the Sultan of Morocco as an independent sovereign, in whose lands all Powers were to hold the same footing and enjoy the same commercial rights[2]. This was to ignore the French claim to exercise a certain measure of administrative control in Morocco, especially in the parts bordering

[1] Tardieu, *La France et les Alliances*, p. 205; Reventlow, pp. 228–233.
[2] Tardieu, *La France et les Alliances*, pp. 207–9.

Algeria—a claim which Great Britain and Spain had recognised and approved.

Now, Germany had certainly grounds for annoyance[1]. But the question arises—Why did she veil that annoyance and take no action until March 1905? The answer is clear. Her action was based on the fact that Russia, and therefore France, were now weak. While the Franco-Russian Alliance retained its original strength, Germany said not a word about Morocco. She bided her time; and, so soon as the opportunity came, she shot her bolt. The German historian Rachfahl admits this. He says: "Because under the surface of the Morocco affair lurked "the deepest and most difficult problems of power (*Macht-* "*probleme*), it was to be foreseen that its course would "prove to be a trial of strength of the first order[2]."

That is quite true. The importance of the Morocco question does not lie in the details. It is easy to wander about among them and miss the significance of the whole affair. German writers and newspaper editors at once declared it to be a trial of strength between Germany and Austria on the one side, and Great Britain and France on the other. Italy and Russia stood outside the ring. The question therefore was whether the Anglo-French Entente would prove to be solid; or would go to pieces at the first shock. Germany intended to show that she was not going to be pushed out of world-politics, or, in the words of the Kaiser (July 3, 1900): "The ocean "reminds us that neither on it nor across it in the distance "can any great decision be again arrived at without "Germany and the German Emperor."

[1] E. D. Morel, *Morocco in Diplomacy*, chs. XI–XIII.
[2] F. Rachfahl, *Kaiser und Reich* (Berlin, 1913), p. 233.

Germany was not about to be pushed out from Morocco. Her interests there were purely commercial, as her Chancellor admitted; and those interests were guaranteed. Moreover, at that time her trade with Morocco (though fast increasing) could not compare in volume with that of Great Britain or France. If, therefore, she chose to consider Morocco as of vital importance to her, it must have been for wider reasons, which were not far to seek. Firstly, the statesmen of Berlin hoped to shatter the Anglo-French compact at the very point which had clinched it, viz. Morocco. But, secondly, the German navy badly needed coaling-stations. Between the North Sea and Togoland and the Cameroons was a very long space which she wished to halve by some intermediate station. In Morocco—say at Mogador or Agadir—such a station could be found. And if France, England, and Spain really intended to partition Morocco, Germany had some right to expect compensation in one of those towns. That was seen from the outset. Therefore, not only was the Morocco Question a *Machtfrage* for the purpose of testing the Anglo-French Entente, but also of procuring a much needed coaling-station. Here one must admit the fatality of Germany. Coming last into the field of World-Policy, she could not acquire a coaling-station without alarming everybody. France, Great Britain, Spain, and above all the United States were annoyed; for Mogador or Agadir, would be half way to South Brazil; and South Brazil is under the shield of the Monroe Doctrine.

The intervention of the Kaiser in Morocco lost nothing by the language of his ambassadors. It was well known at Paris, and therefore at Berlin, that France was not ready for war; that alone, without the help of Russia, she was sure to succumb. M. Rouvier, President of the Council of Ministers, admitted as much in the Chamber of Deputies during the humiliating debate of April 19, 1905, which may be termed the analogue of the debate of mid-July before the present crisis. A special envoy of the German Government, Prince Henckel von Donnersmarck, came to Paris and spoke as a Jupiter tonans. He said that it was now clear that the Anglo-French Entente had been framed for the isolation and humiliation of Germany. Was the recent Moroccan policy that of France or of her Foreign Minister? The policy of that Minister was aimed at the Germans, who would not wait until it was completed. It was also the policy of England to destroy the fleet of every rival, or better still, to prevent its construction. But could the British fleet help France? That fleet might bombard German towns and destroy German commerce. None the less, the milliards which Germany would wring from France would rebuild both towns and merchantmen. Let France think better of it. Give up the Minister who had made the trouble, and adopt towards Germany a loyal and open policy, such as would guarantee the peace of the world[1].

This remarkable pronouncement disclosed the real motives of the Court of Berlin. They were intended, not so much to promote the attainment of German aims in Morocco, as to give a brutal demonstration of the worthlessness of the Anglo-French Entente when contrasted with the might of Germany. The purpose was to separate Great Britain and France, not to secure commercial concessions.

[1] Substance of a conversation printed by *le Gaulois* (June, 1905).

The upshot was that France decided to sacrifice Delcassé. There is no doubt that he had pushed ahead too far and too fast. His resignation, which took place on June 12, 1905, was desirable; but that it should take place at the imperious dictation of Germany was a Pyrrhic triumph for the victor. It enraged everyone. France ground her teeth and thought more than ever of revenge. Great Britain, no less than France, felt the blow dealt at Paris; and Russia knew full well that Muscovite defeats in Manchuria accounted for the whole affair. For the time the *Realpolitik* of Berlin succeeded, but only at the cost of exasperating three Great Powers; and such a success is really defeat. All three Powers began to take precautions for the future; and Europe became more than ever an armed camp. France had been alarmed by Germany's threats; and in the latter part of 1905 voted the sum of £60,000,000 to make good the defects in her army organisation, including more than a million for strategic railways[1]. The retort of Germany was sharp and highly significant. In 1906 she commenced, among other things, the construction of a system of strategic railways from the Rhine, about Cologne, towards the Belgian frontier. Those railways, running through a rather sparsely inhabited country, aroused suspicion at the time. Only in this year has their terrible motive been fully revealed.

That Germany's chief aim throughout was to separate France from Great Britain and from Russia appeared clearly enough during the Algesiras Conference (Jan.— March 1906). But she failed. Her efforts were marked by too much of Teutonic vigour, so much so that on one

[1] Tardieu, *op. cit.* p. 229.

occasion (March 17, 1906) they alienated the sympathy
even of Mr Roosevelt. Though plied by the Kaiser
with three personal telegrams, the President of the United
States replied that he found the German propositions
unacceptable. They were so to all the Powers, and
finally, on March 26, Germany had to give way and
accept the compromise proposed by the French plenipotentiaries. The policy of Berlin had in turn gone
counter to that of Italy, Russia, the United States, and
even of Austria. This diplomatic defeat clearly resulted
from excess of confidence or excess of zeal. Oscar Wilde
once said that nothing succeeds like excess. That may
be true in up-to-date literature; doubtless, it is true
for the modern theatre; but it is not true in the diplomatic
sphere. There the advice of Talleyrand to a beginner
is always applicable: "*Et surtout pas trop de zèle.*"

The most important result of the Algesiras Conference
remains to be noticed—the Anglo-Russian Entente.
That understanding between the former deadly rivals
would have appeared either miraculous or monstrous to
men of the time of Beaconsfield. But it is now fairly
clear that Russia took seriously to heart the lessons of
the Japanese War and saw the folly of that aggressive
policy which had earned the distrust of all her neighbours.
For the time she was amenable to reason, and Germany
was not. That was the outstanding lesson of the Conference of Algesiras. British and Russian diplomatists
there discovered ground for common action. Therefore
that happened which always will happen when a Great
Power tries to give the law to the others. They drew
nearer together for mutual support. This has ever been
the outcome of *Weltpolitik*—that of Philip II of Spain, of

Louis XIV, of Napoleon, of Wilhelm II. The last-named has succeeded, firstly, in making the British lion lie down by the side of the Russian bear, and, secondly, in rousing them to joint action. It is his chief diplomatic achievement.

Some years earlier, viz. in 1900–1, a British writer, evidently a diplomat, had maintained in the pages of the *Fortnightly Review* that we ought to come to terms with Russia. But at that time it seemed a mere dream. Then came the Dogger Bank incident, when we were on the brink of war with Russia. But Morocco and Algesiras ended all that. After the close of the Japanese War, the Tsar let it be known that he desired friendly relations with Great Britain; and he received Sir Charles Hardinge in a markedly cordial manner at St Petersburg[1]. Algesiras having furthered the entente, Sir Edward Grey admitted on May 24, 1906, that, though there was no definite accord between Great Britain and Russia, yet they were more and more inclined to discuss amicably all the questions at issue between them. In March, 1907, a Russian Squadron received a hearty welcome at our naval ports; and in the month of August following the two Powers came to an agreement respecting Persia, Afghanistan, and Thibet[2]. It is impossible here to enter into details, save that Central Asian questions have since that time ceased to trouble us as they did in former periods. For a time tranquillity in Central Asia seemed to be dearly bought at the cost of our concurrence in Russia's Persian policy; but that is now seen to be a side issue compared with the graver questions at stake in Europe.

[1] *The Times*, October 23, 1905.   [2] Tardieu, 282–6.

In 1909 there appeared for a time a prospect of better
relations with Germany; and the improvement was
almost certainly due to the personal intervention of
H.M. Edward VII. During a State visit to Berlin he
discussed important matters, thus probably helping on
the Franco-German agreement on the Moroccan Question
which was signed at Berlin on Feb. 9, 1909[1]. France
thereby recognised the integrity of Morocco; while
Germany admitted that France should maintain order
in the interior. The agreement obviously was vague;
and it soon fell through owing to the outbreak of disturbances in that land.

Accordingly, in the early summer of 1911, France
sent an expedition to Fez, whereupon Spain occupied
points on the West coast, allotted to her by the secret
Franco-Spanish treaty of 1904. Germany, seeing her
commercial interests threatened, made protests; and
when nothing came of them, sent the corvette *Panther* to
Agadir (July 1911) in order "to help and protect German
"subjects and clients in those regions." Much could be
said in favour of some such step, for as matters then stood,
German interests were certain to suffer unless she made
a stand against French and Spanish expansion in Morocco.
But the Pan-Germans aggravated the crisis by demanding
the annexation of all S.W. Morocco; and no less a person
than the Secretary of State, Kiderlen-Wächter, declared
privately that the German flag would never be hauled
down at Agadir, and that he would not hear of any
exchange of it for French Congo districts[2].

---

[1] Rachfahl, p. 310; Reventlow, p. 309; Pinon, 185.

[2] See article in the *Fortnightly Review*, xci (new series, 462) founded,
in part, on revelations made on oath by Herr Class, President of the

British Ministers protested against the action of Germany; and it was made clear that her occupation of Agadir and its coast was an unfriendly act, respecting which Great Britain must be consulted. The silence of Germany respecting this declaration led to a shrill remonstrance from Mr Lloyd George; and the whole affair trended dangerously near to war. The secrets of that time have not been disclosed; and we cannot expect to fathom the motives of the Kaiser with any approach to certainty; but it is generally believed that he desired to avert war. The anonymous author of that curious book, "The Secrets of the German War Office," asserts that the German war party intended by the despatch of the *Panther* to provoke a quarrel with Great Britain or France; also that peace was maintained only by the personal interposition of the Kaiser, who sent him, a secret agent of the Government, with the utmost haste and secrecy to Agadir. His mission was to warn the captain of the *Panther* that in no circumstances was he to begin hostilities with the French and British vessels in that port. The statement is made without proof and is on several grounds suspicious. Nevertheless, if not true to fact, it is true to character. The Kaiser appears to have desired peace.

It is, however, doubtful whether his pacific leanings were due to a persistent conviction, or whether he desired to defer a rupture until a more favourable juncture. Was

Pan-German League. Reventlow (p. 354) asserts that Kiderlen–Wächter always looked to an exchange between S.W. Morocco and districts on the French Congo, such as finally was arranged. But this seems a lame excuse for the final compromise, which the Pan-Germans detested.

he waiting for a time when the Kiel Canal would be
widened so as to admit the German Dreadnoughts then in
course of construction? And was he dismayed at the
prospect of the huge financial crash which bankers and
merchants confidently prophesied as the immediate
result of war? On both grounds it was highly desirable
to avert hostilities. Then, too, in the Bosnian Crisis of
1908–9 (see Lecture VI) he had inflicted a rebuff on the
Powers of the Triple Entente; and after strengthening
his control over the Turkish Empire, he might hope
before long to find in the re-organised Turkish army an
effective ally against Russia in Caucasia, and England in
Egypt.

For these reasons—naval, diplomatic, and financial—
it is highly probable that the Kaiser's resolve not to
provoke a rupture in 1911 was based on prudential considerations. As events have actually shown, the Triple
Entente was stronger in 1914 that in 1911. But that
could not have been foreseen. According to all appear-
ances in 1911, the Kaiser might well deem that the Triple
Alliance would be stronger, and the Triple Entente
weaker, in the near future; and this result would have
come about but for that unexpected event in the autumn
of 1911—Italy's attack upon Turkey, which will be
considered in due course[1].

It is now time to turn to the Bagdad Railway Question,
which closely concerns the future of Asia Minor, Mesopotamia, and Egypt. The scheme crystallized in 1898 at
the time of the Kaiser's visit to the Holy Land. Out-

[1] For the final settlement of the Moroccan Question see E. D. Morel,
op. cit. pp. 304–323, also the cessions of the French Congo territory to
Germany.

wardly he appeared as a crusader, championing the
interests of Christian pilgrims to Jerusalem, for whom
he gained concessions from the Sultan[1]. But he also
procured from the Sultan a verbal promise for the construction of the Bagdad Railway. This happened in
the year succeeding the Armenian and Macedonian
massacres. At the time of those outbreaks of calculating
fanaticism strong remonstrances were made to the
Sublime Porte by the Western Powers. They were
fruitless. For many years past Germany had supported
Turkey, in pursuance of the policy of Prussia traditional
since the days of Frederick the Great; and in 1897
Kaiser William emphasized the closeness of the political
tie connecting the German and Ottoman Empires[2].
Consequently poets and idealists in Western Europe
raged in vain against the atrocities perpetrated by " Abdul
Hamid the Damned." The power behind his throne
was the Kaiser, who found his reward for the great betrayal
of 1897 in the bargain for the Bagdad Railway. In
1902 the Porte issued a firman authorising that enterprise.

The Kaiser, during his visit to these shores in November,
1902, probably sought to interest our Government in
his scheme. True, Mr Balfour denied that we were
asked to participate in it, and scolded the *Spectator* for
crediting that story. But early in 1903 General von
der Goltz delivered to the Königsberg Geographical
Society a lecture in which he stated that the German
Bagdad Syndicate had secured a concession for extending

[1] Elkind, *The German Emperor's Speeches* (pp. 62–4, 318–322):
" Not splendour, not power, not glory, not honour, no earthly blessing
is it that we seek here: we pine, we pray, we strive alone after the sole,
the highest blessing, the salvation of our souls."

[2] Sir H. Rumbold, *Final Recollections of a Diplomatist*, p. 296.

its line to Koweit on the Persian Gulf "after diplomatic "negotiations with Great Britain[1]." He also foretold that British mails for India would soon go viâ Vienna, Constantinople, Bagdad, and Koweit. It was evident that British trade in the Persian Gulf, especially at Basra, would largely be diverted to this railway, especially if, as was contemplated, it was connected with European lines by a tunnel under the Bosphorus. In this case, there would be through communication from Ostend or Antwerp to the Persian Gulf, with serious results to our shipping interests.

But the promoters of the German Bagdad scheme showed clearly enough that political and military issues of great moment were at stake. This appeared in a work, *Die Bagdadbahn*, published in 1902 by Dr P. Rohrbach, whose travels in Mesopotamia, originating in theological motives, had of late led him to take a decidedly militant tone. He stated frankly that it was not worth while spending a pfennig for a weak Turkey; but for a strong Turkey it might be worth while to spend many million marks. He pointed out how the Bagdad Railway would enable the Sublime Porte to bring up its Anatolian troops quickly to the Bosphorus, whereas in the Russo-Turkish War of 1876-7 seven months were wasted by the troops from Mesopotamia before arrival at the front. The new lines would double the military strength of the Ottoman Empire. Further, the prosperity of Mesopotamia and Asia Minor would revive, stimulated as it would be by the immigration of numbers of Germans. Thus, both in a financial and military sense Turkey would soon

---

[1] See the *Spectator* for November 8, 1902, April 4, 1903; also June 5, 1909, and *Nineteenth Century and After*, June, 1909.

be able to resist her redoubtable enemy, Russia. Rohrbach also affirmed that agreements had been almost
secured both with France and with Great Britain (this,
too, in 1902).

The revival of irrigation in Mesopotamia was already
planned by Sir William Wilcocks; but the arrival of
the Bagdad Railway might have helped the development
of that now desolate region. Nevertheless, in view of
the unfriendly conduct of Germany in other quarters,
the Bagdad scheme had to be scrutinised closely. Her
ambassador at Constantinople, Baron Marschall von
Bieberstein, was openly hostile to Great Britain; and,
if we had helped on the Bagdad scheme, we should at
once have been represented as the enemies of Russia.
On the other hand the British opposition to the Bagdad
scheme was finally declared by a German writer in the
Nineteenth Century and After [June, 1909] to be due
to Russian instigation. Clearly, the only way with so
intricate and compromising a scheme was to let it alone,
and allow the Germans to make the line if they could
get the money for it. They failed to carry through
the original scheme so far as concerned the Persian
Gulf. To this extension the British Government could
not assent; for it would have enabled Turkey and
Germany to send troops quickly to the confines of Persia,
and a further extension of the line would threaten India.
The design of Germany and Austria to control the Balkan
Peninsula and Asia Minor appeared clearly in the years
1908–10. In 1908 Austria annexed Bosnia; and though
for a time in that year the Young Turk Movement overthrew German influence at Constantinople, yet the
intrigues of Baron von Marschall brought about a complete

revival of Teutonic ascendancy in April 1909. Ever since
that time the Young Turks have been the creatures of
Berlin. All the more reason, then, had we for opposing
the German scheme of " pacific penetration " to the
Persian Gulf, where British merchants had long before
built up an extremely valuable trade[1]. Moreover, the
terminus, Koweit, was the city of an independent Sheikh
whom we had more than once supported against the
coercion of Abdul-Hamid. In 1911 Sir Edward Grey
demanded that, if a railway were made to the Gulf, it
must be a purely commercial undertaking. Herein he
followed the lines laid down by Lord Lansdowne, who
stated that we could never allow another Power to obtain
there a strong naval position " which might be used on
" the flank of our communications with India."

Such an assertion was all the more needed because
of a recent compact between Russia and Germany.
In November, 1910, the Tsar visited the Kaiser at Potsdam
and they conferred together on matters of State. Their
meeting caused no little surprise in view of the rebuff
which the Kaiser had dealt to the Tsar in the winter of
1908–9 over the Bosnian Question. It now seemed that
the Tsar had accepted defeat and was willing to follow
the lead of Germany. The meeting of the two Emperors
therefore caused great concern at London and Paris;
for it might betoken the break-up of the Triple Entente,
lately severely strained by the death of H.M. Edward VII.
The German account of the deliberations of the two
Emperors is as follows: Russia agreed not to oppose
the scheme, and even to lihk up that railway with her
Persian lines; also to recognize Germany as an equal

[1] D. Fraser, *The Short Cut to India* (1909), chs. 19–25.

in matters commercial in that country. The Court of
Berlin, on its side, recognized that Russia had special
political and strategic interests in Northern Persia, as
well as rights to construct railways, roads, and telegraphs.
Thus, Germany said in effect, "Help me to build the
"Bagdad Railway through to the Persian Gulf, and I
"will hand over to you North Persia and as much of
"that land as you want." But this was not all. The
Russian and German Governments also gave mutual
assurances that each would enter into no engagement
inimical to the other[1].

The Potsdam Convention was a triumph for the
diplomacy of Germany. She had set back Russia's
interests at the time of the Bosnian crisis; and she pushed
on the Bagdad Railway until it promised to become
a menace to Russian Caucasia. Then she turned round
and said, "Now that I have beaten you, will you not
"make a bargain? Let us virtually partition Persia
"between us, shutting out the British; and, while we
"are about it, let us have a friendly understanding all
"round. I will not attack you in any quarter, if you
"will not attack me." The method is rather crude,
as German diplomacy has been since Bismarck's day.
It succeeded in 1910. But it seems probable that the
Potsdam compact marks the last success of this policy
of blows and bluff.

For the time there were searchings of heart at London
and Paris. Was the Triple Entente of any avail if Russia
could thus clasp the hand of our declared rival? And
were there any secret clauses? Such were the questions

[1] Raohfahl, pp. 331–2; *Nineteenth Century and After*, June, 1914,
pp. 1323–6,

that agitated the political world[1]. Obviously, the year 1911 was one of great anxiety for French and British statesmen; and the facts just passed in review explain why the war party at Berlin so vehemently clamoured for hostilities with France and Great Britain at the time of the Agadir affair.

Their confidence found expression in several ways. Germany had recently gained from the Sultan a concession respecting the port of Alexandretta which made it for all practical purposes a German port. She also secured permission to build an important branch line to Damascus and past the east of the Dead Sea and the Sinaitic Peninsula to Mecca. It comes almost within striking distance of the Suez Canal. Represented as a semi-philanthropic enterprise, designed to lessen the hardships of pilgrims proceeding to Mecca, it was always intended to menace Egypt. This was stated by Dr Rohrbach in a later edition of his book (1911):

England can be attacked and mortally wounded by land from Europe only in one place—Egypt. The loss of Egypt would mean for England not only the end of her dominion over the Suez Canal, and of her connections with India and the Far East, but would probably entail the loss of her possessions in Central and East Africa. The conquest of Egypt by a Mohammedan Power, like Turkey, would also imperil England's hold over her 60,000,000 Mohammedan subjects in India, besides prejudicing her relations with Afghanistan and Persia. Turkey, however, can never dream of recovering Egypt until she is mistress of a developed railway system in Asia Minor and Syria, and until, through the progress of the Anatolian Railway to Bagdad, she is in a position to withstand an attack by England upon Mesopotamia.... Egypt is a prize which

---

[1] See an article in *La Revue des Questions diplomatiques* (Jan.–June, 1911) which reproaches Russia with her Persian policy, which "a émasculé la Triple Entente."

for Turkey would be well worth the risk of taking sides with
Germany in a war with England. The policy of protecting
Turkey, which is now pursued by Germany, has no object but
the desire to effect an insurance against the danger of a war
with England.

The Bagdad-Mecca scheme aimed at the revival of
the Moslem Power[1]; and that Power, when strengthened
by German money, and drilled by German officers, was
to play a great part in an eventual conflict with Russia
or Great Britain. The curious tactics of the *Goeben*
and the *Breslau*, and the coercion recently employed
by Germany at Constantinople, explain the drift of events
in the Near East. The Kaiser and his Ministers supported
successively the Sultan and the Young Turks against
the impulse for reform because they saw in the Ottoman
Empire an effective ally against Russia and a means
of dealing a deadly blow at a vital part of the British
Empire.

It may be asked—How could the Kaiser make the
mistake of hoping to dominate Egypt without previously
having gained the mastery at sea? Does not Bonaparte's
adventure of 1798 stand as a warning against such an
attempt? Not wholly, I think. For the Corsican
committed two blunders, firstly, of not securing the
definite support of Turkey before he sought to overthrow the Mamelukes; secondly, of disregarding British
maritime power at a time when sea-power counted for

[1] It proved very profitable to the promoters and burdensome to
Ottoman finance: see D. Fraser, *op. cit.* chs. II–V, XVIII; L. Fraser,
articles in *National Review*, April, May, 1911; Mons. A Géraud, in
articles in *Nineteenth Century and After*, May, June, 1914, shows the
weakness of the Anglo-French opposition to the scheme. On the Homs-
Bagdad railway scheme, favoured by England and France, which utterly
failed, see *The Imperial and Asiatic Quarterly* (July, 1912).

far more than it does in the present case. Bonaparte's exploit was therefore doomed to failure, if we and the Turks attacked him. Now, however, in favourable circumstances, the Kaiser and the Turks might attack Egypt with a fair chance of success. For he and they reckoned on having almost continuous communications by land between Berlin and the Sinaitic Peninsula. If Balkan affairs had gone as he desired, Austria would have controlled the line to Constantinople, and have poured troops speedily into Syria, thence menacing the Suez Canal. There only could the Sea-Power have opposed any effective resistance; and it is doubtful whether warships cooped up in a canal can long oppose with success an attack of a large army provided with pontoons. We shall do well not to underrate the danger at the canal, though it is far less formidable than was designed at Berlin, Vienna, and Constantinople. For, as we shall see in Lecture VI, neither Italy nor the little peoples of the Balkans maintained the passive rôle which the Kaiser desired. They successively attacked Turkey, thereby enfeebling her and preventing that through railway communication with Syria which was needed for the full realization of the dreams of the modern Alexander the Great.

LECTURE V

ALSACE-LORRAINE

La conquête et l'annexion par la force de l'Alsace et de la Lorraine sont le principal obstacle à la paix et la vraie cause des armaments gigantesques.

(La Ligue internationale de la Paix. Geneva, 1884.)

IN nearly all wars there are motives deeper and more fundamental than those which appear on the surface. The latter may be the occasion of the rupture, but they need not be the fundamental cause. It is so in the present instance. The murder of the Archduke Francis Ferdinand was merely the spark that ignited vast stores of combustible material which had long been accumulating. They may be classed in three general groups. The first was due to the clash of British and German national interests, especially in matters colonial and naval. This we have already surveyed. But that friction might have continued indefinitely, had not flames burst forth in the south-east of Europe. The flames spread swiftly to France (and incidentally to Belgium) because France was on the same electrical circuit as Russia. When we inquire why the French Republic is connected with the Tsardom, we find the cause in the deep-lying hatred and fear of Germany

which has prevailed at Paris since the year 1870. Those
feelings centre in the Alsace-Lorraine Question, which,
as by an electric thrill, set the West in a blaze so soon
as fire broke forth in the East.

In September, 1870, during the Franco-German War,
when the first feelers with regard to peace were put
forth by the young French Republic to the victors,
Bismarck declared that Germany must have Strassburg
and Metz. To German diplomatists he wrote, " So long
" as France possesses Strassburg and Metz, her strategical
" position is stronger offensively than ours is defensively.
" ....In Germany's possession, Strassburg and Metz
" assume a defensive aspect. In more than twenty
" wars with France we have never been the aggressors.
" We have nothing to demand from her except our
" own security....From Germany no disturbance of
" the peace of Europe need be feared[1]." These words
constituted a pledge that the possession of Alsace and
part of Lorraine would be a guarantee for the peace of
the world. From the historical standpoint Bismarck was
right. With the exception of Metz and its district,
Alsace-Lorraine belonged to Germany by right of ancient
possession. It was partly by force, partly by fraud,
that Louis XIV acquired Strassburg and neighbouring
towns. Further, the German plea was tenable on military
grounds. Under the two Napoleons France had recklessly
disturbed the peace of Europe; and we are suffering
now from the final results of the Napoleonic policy.
The recollections of the times of the two Emperors still
haunt the brain of Germany and indispose her to any
weakening of her Western frontier.

[1] Lowe, *Prince Bismarck*, I. 568; Sir R. Morier. *Memoirs*, II. 220–9.

But what of the sentiments of the Alsatians and Lorrainers? Did they incline towards France or Germany? Here there was little doubt. Ever since the great Revolution, Alsace-Lorraine had been enthusiastically French. That great event sent a thrill through those once German provinces and united them with *la patrie*; witness the declaration of the deputies of Lorraine at that memorable sitting of the National Assembly on August 4, 1789. After Dauphiné, Brittany, and other provinces had renounced their local privileges, the men of Lorraine stood up and declared that their province, though the youngest of all, desired to join intimately the life of "this glorious family." Alsace-Lorraine sealed those sentiments with their blood in the Revolutionary and Napoleonic Wars, when Kellermann, Kléber, Ney, Rapp, and many others added lustre to the French arms. Thenceforth those provinces were French to the core.

Early in 1871 Bismarck had an uneasy feeling that the annexation of the French-speaking districts of Lorraine about Metz might be undesirable. His secretary, Busch, reports him as saying, "If they (the French) gave us " a milliard more, we might perhaps let them have Metz. " We would then take 800,000,000 francs and build " ourselves a fortress a few miles further back....I do " not like so many Frenchmen being in our house against " their will. It is just the same with Belfort. It is all " French there too. The military men, however, will not " be willing to let Metz slip, and perhaps they are right[1]."

It is well known that Bismarck and Moltke differed sharply on this subject. Moltke kept saying that the

[1] Busch, *Bismarck in the Franco-German War*, II. 341; *Journals of Count von Blumenthal*, pp. 316–8 (Eng. edit.).

acquisition of Metz meant a difference of 100,000 men
in a campaign; and this estimate convinced the Emperor
William[1]. Probably the Germans had from the outset
resolved to have Alsace-Lorraine; for they imposed
German institutions immediately after military occupation, a step which they did not take in districts further
West. At the first mention of the terms of peace
the 35 deputies of the doomed lands made a strong
protest to the French Chambers, then at Bordeaux:
" Alsace and Lorraine refuse to be alienated. With one
" voice, the citizens at their firesides, the soldiers under
" arms, the former by voting, the latter by fighting,
" proclaim to Germany and to the world at large, the
" immutable will of Alsace and Lorraine to remain
" French. France can neither consent to nor sign the
" cession of Lorraine and Alsace without imperilling
" the continuity of her national existence, and, with
" her own hands dealing a death-blow to her unity[2]."

That was the opinion of nearly all Alsatians and
Lorrainers. But Germany held them in her grip except the
maiden fortress of Belfort. Further, Bismarck was ordered
by his sovereign not to relax his terms. M. Thiers, however,
made a supreme appeal to prevent the annexation of
Belfort. Failing even at that point to break the will
of the iron Chancellor, he broke forth into the following
protest: " Well then. Let it be as you will, Count!
" These negotiations are nothing but a sham....Make
" war, then. Ravage our provinces, burn our houses,
" slaughter the inoffensive inhabitants: complete your

[1] Blowitz, *My Memoirs*, p. 161.

[2] J. Simon, *The Government of M. Thiers* (Eng. trans.), I. 129, 130;
H. Welschinger, *La Protestation de l'Alsace-Lorraine* (Paris, 1914).

" work. We will fight you until our last breath. We
" may be defeated, but at least we shall not be dis-
" honoured." Even Bismarck was moved. He retired
to consult, first Moltke and then his sovereign; and the
verdict was that France should retain Belfort, provided
that the Germans should enter Paris in triumph. The
proud city underwent that humiliation with quiet disdain
because she saved Belfort.

At the last moment it seemed that Bismarck would
break off the negotiations. On February 25 he spoke
with extreme harshness to the French plenipotentiaries
and accused them of spinning out the conferences. The
cause of his anger was obvious. The British Government
was about to make representations concerning the
enormous indemnity claimed by Germany from France.
That sum had been fixed at six milliards (£240,000,000).
But on February 23 the Emperor William consented
to reduce it to five milliards (£200,000,000)[1]. Whether
this reduction was due to the generosity of the old
Emperor or to a knowledge that Great Britain was
about to take diplomatic action, is open to question.
Certainly, here was one cause of the extreme anger of
Bismarck and the German Headquarters against us.

But there were other causes. Some of our manufacturers had secretly supplied munitions of war to the
French, a fact which the German Staff ascertained and
forthwith proclaimed to the four winds. Secondly, a
portion of the British Press indulged in unseemly diatribes
against the Germans for their harshness in the conduct
of the war and in the demand for Alsace-Lorraine[2].

---

[1] J. Simon, *The Government of M. Thiers* (Eng. transl.), I. 137.
[2] Sir R. Morier, *Memoirs*, II. 165, 246.

The German newspapers savagely retorted, and thus there began that ceaseless war of words which must be pronounced an indirect but important cause of this war. When journalists of all lands learn the urgent need of self-restraint in times of general excitement, the cause of peace will take a long stride forward.

Bismarck also inveighed against the British Government for asking permission to send a gunboat up the River Seine in order to remove English refugees. He peremptorily refused, saying that we desired merely to find out whether the Germans had laid mines in the river below Rouen, so that French warships might follow the gunboat. Referring to our real motive (surely, by no means discreditable) he burst out, "What swine! They " are full of vexation and envy because we have fought " great battles here and won them. They cannot bear " to think that shabby little Prussia should prosper so.... " They have always done their utmost to injure us. " The Crown Princess herself is an incarnation of this " way of thinking. She is full of her own great con- " descension in marrying into our country[1]."

The terms imposed by Germany upon France seemed designed to crush her to the earth. Great therefore was the joy at London and the annoyance at Berlin, when, under the fostering care of Thiers, France paid off the enormous war indemnity by the spring of 1873. Thus the Germans had violated the maxim of Frederick the Great, "Never maltreat an enemy by halves." They had deeply wounded France by tearing from her two provinces that formed an integral part of her life. Yet they had not wholly crushed her; and since 1875 they

[1] *Bismarck: Some Secret Pages*, I. 500.

have had no chance of doing so except by an unparalleled effort. That has been a dominant factor of the European situation. Just as the Eastern Question brought Russia and Austria into sharp rivalry, so Alsace-Lorraine kept up an irreconcilable feud between France and Germany; and by degrees the two Germanic Empires ranged themselves together, while France and Russia became close allies.

This arrangement lay in the natural order of things. So far back as 1856 Bismarck had discerned that truth, which became clear after the crisis of 1875[1]. But the Franco-Russian alliance came about slowly owing to his cautious and skilful policy. To this we must briefly advert; for it is not too much to say that his dealings with the Great Powers were prompted by a resolve to escape, if possible, from the consequences of the annexation of Alsace-Lorraine. Foreseeing that France would seek to reconquer those provinces, he sought to keep her isolated.

His first effort was the Three Emperors' League (*Dreikaiserbund*) of 1872. When that compact virtually lapsed in the crisis of 1875, he looked about for an alternative scheme. The crisis in the Eastern Question in 1876–8 gave him his chance. He supported Austrian claims against those of Russia, and thus in 1879 found his reward in the Austro-German alliance. But he did not desire to offend Russia. Both William I and he desired merely to teach Russia a sharp lesson; and, when she had learnt it, in isolation, they would welcome her back. This policy of alternate cudgelling and cajoling led to

[1] Busch, *Our Chancellor*, I. 320.

what have been termed the Reinsurance Treaties with
Russia—a topic too complex for treatment here[1].

Far more important and interesting is the skilful
lead which Bismarck gave to France into the colonial
adventures of the eighties. He sketched their first
outlines at the time of the Berlin Congress of 1878. His
ingenuity at that time would have made Machiavelli
hail him as a master in this craft. While opposing the
oncoming tide of Slavonic "barbarism," he found means
to turn the energies of Great Britain, France, and Italy
towards Africa. Oppert, correspondent of the *Times* at
Berlin, states that Bismarck gave the following advice
to Beaconsfield:—Do not quarrel with Russia. Let her
take Constantinople, while you take Egypt—France will
not prove inexorable. Besides, one might give her
Syria or Tunis[2]. At that time, then, he cared not a jot
for Turkey. He was even desirous of starting a partition
of the Ottoman Empire, provided that the German
Empire thereby gained immunity from a similar proceeding
—witness his graphic declaration, that the whole Eastern
Question was not worth the bones of a single Pomeranian
grenadier.

His foresight was justified. France in 1880 began
to cast jealous eyes upon Tunis, which Italy had marked
out for herself; and when the statesmen of Rome plied
M. de Freycinet at Paris with anxious questions, they
could gain from him no more assuring reply than that
" for the present, France had no intention of occupying
" Tunis, but that the future was in the hands of God."

---

[1] See J. W. Headlam, *Bismarck*, pp. 442, 443.
[2] *Ibid.* II. 92; Blowitz, *My Memoirs*, p. 165; Crispi, *Memoirs*,
vol. II. pp. 98.

A little later, when Rome became more restive, Freycinet gave up his predestinarian argument and said plainly, " Why will you persist in thinking of Tunis?....Why " not turn your attention to Tripoli?" Bismarck's procedure is worth noting: Great Britain is directed towards Egypt; France towards Tunis; and she, in order to " square " Italy, waves her on to Tripoli. The Chancellor contrived the scheme; but the statesmen of Paris, London, and finally of Rome concurred in it[1].

By this gigantic " deal " in North Africa Bismarck diverted political activity away from Europe to the Dark Continent. What was more, he set by the ears not only French and Britons but French and Italians. During twenty-two years (1882–1904) we were on strained terms with France respecting Egypt. Further, the Sultan Abdul Hamid never forgave us for our intervention in Egypt; and the Pan-Islam movement which that crafty potentate so skilfully nursed was largely the outcome of our presence in that land. True, we went to Egypt in 1882 as the mandatories of Europe to secure order; but we went with the ostensible blessings and secret curses of the Balaam of Berlin. As for the feud between France and Italy respecting Tunis, it survived to the year 1911, when Italy acquired Tripoli. Until then, she could not feel cordially towards the French, who had played her that shabby trick over Tunis in 1881.

During many years the energies of France obeyed the centrifugal impulse which Bismarck had skilfully imparted. Some of her ministers, notably M. Ferry, suffered from colony-fever. France seemed for the time to have forgotten Alsace-Lorraine amidst these distant

[1] Crispi, *Mems.* II. pp. 97–104.

quests. But at the end of the year 1885 a reaction
set in. Tens of thousands of French youths had perished
of malaria amidst the swamps of Tonquin or the forests
of Madagascar; and M. Clémenceau and other patriots
asked indignantly what had France to show for this
waste of life and treasure—Great Britain offended,
China hostile, and Germany cynically complacent. He
pointed his attacks by assertions, culled from the German
Press, that the French were the inferiors of the Germans,
and that the Republic was much in the debt of the
Teutonic Empire for helping on her colonial enterprises.
The elections of 1885 sent up a large number of royalist
and Bonapartist deputies. It was clear that the Republic
would fall if it persevered in plunging into tropical swamps;
and it came very near to perishing at the time of the
Boulanger crisis. *Le brav' général*, who caracolled about
Paris on his black charger, was in reality a poor creature[1].
He became a danger to the Republic chiefly because
he championed a national policy. For this he was
abused by the German Press, a fact which gained him
the heart of France. He rode on the crest of public
opinion because he bade Frenchmen think of Alsace-
Lorraine and prepare for revenge. The first definite
sign of a *rapprochement* between France and Russia
belongs to this year, the year when Russia first renewed
her Reinsurance Treaty with Germany. At the request
of the Court of Petrograd the French Republic undertook to send thither 500,000 Lebel rifles, on the express
stipulation that they should never be used against
France[2].

[1] Sir T. Barclay, *Anglo-French Reminiscences* (1876–1906), p. 96.
[2] Count Reventlow, *Deutschlands auswärtige Politik* (1888–1913), p. 5.

The thought of revenge was kept alive in France by events in the conquered provinces; and to these we must now turn. The North Germans, for all their vigour and manliness, have not the arts that conciliate the vanquished. That was seen clearly by a German Liberal, named Rasch, who in 1876 sought to discover the real state of affairs in the Reichsland (Alsace-Lorraine). He found it absolutely different from what the German newspapers represented. Having had their orders, they described the revival of old German ways, and the popular rejoicings at events such as the starting of a steamboat service, or the opening of the new University buildings at Strassburg. This latter event was recounted in moving terms. But Rasch found that less than one-fourth of the students were natives of the province, and those chiefly theological students who had to study there in order to obtain cures in that Reichsland. The population had dwindled, no fewer than 100,000 having emigrated to France. Metz had sunk from 50,000 to 33,000 inhabitants. This was not surprising; for freedom of the Press was a thing of the past, and the French language was proscribed. In fact, the Germans were hated in the Reichsland[1].

Bismarck had bidden the Alsatians and Lorrainers consider themselves an independent Republic. In reality the Reichsland resembled a satrapy of Xerxes rather than Athens. Our diplomatist, Sir Robert Morier, during a visit to Strassburg in 1872, had an interview with the ex-mayor, a chemist named Klein, who had not been hostile to the German occupation. Klein went

---

[1] E. Rasch, *Die Preussen in Elsass-Lothringen* (1876), chs. II.–V. E. Hinzelin, *L'Alsace sous le Joug* (1914), ch. 11.

with a deputation to Berlin in May, 1871, to beg Bismarck
to defer the imposition of military conscription; but
the Chancellor opposed an adamantine opposition,
because " Prussia had an immense experience of the
"results produced by wearing the Prussian uniform.
" Get the King's coat on to a man's back and let him
" wear it for three years, and you have made not only
" a good soldier but a good citizen of him.... ' Yes ' (was
" Klein's reply), ' but you must get the coat on first,
" and that is what you will not succeed in doing.' "
Bismarck, however, was inexorable; and the results
were that vast numbers of Alsacians, who might have
become reconciled if Germany had treated them with
forbearance, became permanently embittered. Some
12,000 of them fled to France and joined the French
army rather than don the Prussian uniform.

The men of Berlin were deaf to all appeals. They
adopted a drastic system and then forced it through
at all costs. This spirit has been the curse of Berlin
ever since the days of Frederick William I; but never
has it wrought more far-reaching ill than when applied
by the Iron Chancellor to Alsace-Lorraine. The improvements in the legal system and in the railways of the
Reichsland counted for nothing when accompanied by
this premature rule of the drill-sergeant[1].

The Alsatians were virtually an unfree community,
held down by the sword. They retorted by tabooing
the Prussian officials, and extended this ostracism even
to the new station-masters, so that one of them, failing
to find an Alsatian girl who would marry him, had to
institute a search for a wife in Berlin. Fifty wealthy

[1] Sir R. Morier, *Mems.* II. 264–6, 273–4.

manufacturers left Mühlhausen for France. There and throughout Alsace the people were German in type and generally spoke German, but their hearts were in France. Rasch deemed it essential that Germany should know the truth, which was this: her ways were odious to her new subjects, and she must mend those ways if a reconciliation was to be effected. Alas! The Prussian official is not open to conviction; and though a few changes were made at a later time, *e.g.*, a certain measure of constitutional government, yet they produced little or no effect, because there was no change in the spirit of the administration[1]. The Statthalter, Prince Hohenlohe, in February, 1887, made an almost open bribe to the people that they should have full constitutional rights if they ceased to protest against the German connection and entirely accepted it. Then and then only would the Empire relax its policy[2].

If we look deeper, that is, into the thoughts of Bismarck, what do we find? In April of that year he confessed to Busch that he wished he could adopt the methods of Charlemagne and transplant all the Alsatians and Lorrainers to Posen, and all the Poles of Posen into Alsace[3]. In 1912 a German author, Frymann, in a book termed *Wenn ich der Kaiser wär'*, stated the same thought equally crudely : " We acquired Alsace-Lorraine " because the land is necessary to us in a military sense. " The inhabitants were thrown in.... The constitution of " Alsace-Lorraine should be abolished and its administra- " tion be placed under a Minister with dictatorial powers."

---

[1] M. Leroy, *L'Alsace-Lorraine* (Paris, 1914), chs. I–III.
[2] *Mems. of Prince Hohenlohe*, II. 361.
[3] *Bismarck: Some Secret Pages*, III. 167.

There is the reason why Prussia has never won the
Alsatians. She was not the *alma mater*, but rather
the harsh step-mother.

The friction came near to producing war in 1887,
when the German police on the frontier brutally mal-
treated a French agent, named Schnäbele. The Tsar,
Alexander III, sent to Berlin a remonstrance, and William I
arranged matters reasonably. But the incident proved
that the endeavours of Bismarck to divert the thought
and energy of France to Africa had signally failed.
Accordingly Germany had to act up to his motto—
Toujours en vedette.

This appeared in the first Proclamation to the Army
issued by William II, which sent a shiver of apprehension
through Europe. Its effect was not lessened by a later
declaration respecting Alsace-Lorraine. There having
been suggestions in peace-circles as to the neutralising
of those provinces, the late Emperor Frederick was
mentioned as favouring such a scheme. The young
Kaiser emphatically denied it; and at Frankfurt-on-
the-Oder, when unveiling a statue to Prince Frederick
Charles, he uttered these words: " We would rather
" sacrifice our eighteen army corps and our 42,000,000
" inhabitants on the field of battle than surrender a
" single stone of what my father and Prince Frederick
" Charles gained[1]." That was the official version of
the Kaiser's words; but if we may credit Bismarck,
they were far stronger and more melodramatic. For
Bismarck criticized him for saying " If at last the whole
" nation lies hushed in the silence of death[2]." It soon

---

[1] Elkind, *The German Emperor's Speeches*, p. 17.
[2] *Bismarck: Some Secret Pages*, III. 202.

appeared that the young Kaiser intended to put in force a more rigorous régime in the conquered provinces. French writers agree that the state of affairs under him was worse than under William I, and that the increase of rigour has produced little more than an increase of hatred towards Germany. The merchant classes of Alsace-Lorraine may outwardly appear resigned to the new state of things; but at heart they detest it. The 1,550,000 natives long to be free from the Empire. Only the 300,000 German immigrants are loyal to it[1].

The recrudescence of the Alsace-Lorraine Question under William II would, perhaps, not have led to war if he had continued the Bismarckian policy of complaisance towards Russia. But in 1890 he resolved on drawing closer the bonds with Vienna and loosening those with Petrograd. His reasons for this important step were probably as follows. He knew, from a secret report of a German political agent, that the Russians were deficient both in regard to arms and the railway facilities needful for mobilization of their huge array. The chances, therefore, were that Russia would in no case be able to attack Germany before the year 1895[2], and by that time the Kiel Canal would be open, and thereby double the efficiency of the German fleet. For these reasons William II recked little of Russia. He chose to adhere closely to Austria, gave up all thoughts of a Russian connection, and dismissed Bismarck. This is one explanation of the breach between them. The

---

[1] Hinzelin, E., L'Alsace sous le Joug (1914), ch. 12; J. Claretie, Quarante Ans après (1911); A. Hallays, En flânant (1911); Betham Edwards, Under the German Ban (1914).

[2] M. Harden, Monarchs and Men, p. 143.

other explanations are that the Kaiser insisted on the
prosecution of colonial and naval designs, to which
Bismarck demurred, or that he then disliked the Chancellor's anti-Socialist tendencies. Perhaps all these causes
were operative. In any case, Germany and Russia drifted
apart in 1890; and, on the accession of the present Tsar
in 1894, there was an end of the personal motives which had
for so long kept Russia aloof from the French Republic.
The Franco-Russian alliance soon came about, and it was
patent to all the world in June, 1895, when the French
and Russian fleets steamed together into Kiel harbour
to grace the opening of the Kiel Canal. It was their
way of emphasizing the significance of that pacific undertaking. Thus, the completion of Kaiser William's first
naval programme coincides with the hardening of the
national resistance to his designs both on the east and
west of the German Empire. It is no exaggeration to
say that the cautious policy of Bismarck would somehow
have prevented a Franco-Russian alliance. The Kaiser's
restless and ambitious plans, set forth in flamboyant
speeches, helped on that alliance. The isolation of
Germany, which her publicists ascribe to French, Russian,
or British jealousy, was in all probability due mainly
to the reckless policy of William himself. Napoleon I
always declared the alliances against him to be the
outcome of British gold. It is ever the same story.
The would-be conquerors of the world will not understand,
until too late, that the world must insure itself against
them by alliances.

There was another alternative, that the Kaiser should
win the affections of the Alsatians and Lorrainers. He
has tried to do so by methods successful in North Germany.

He has dazzled them by parades. He has re-built in Lorraine a castle which recalls the splendours of old Germany. But he has not won the hearts of that people. Strive as he might, sometimes by menace, sometimes by cajolery, he could not escape from the consequence of the blunder of 1871. The young generation of Alsatians proved to be more Gallophile than that which lived through the war of 1870. Consequently, German policy was held as in a vice. The more the Kaiser fumed and threatened, the closer became the union between France and Russia. The harder he pressed upon the conquered provinces, the more they turned towards Paris. There were but two ways of escape from the deadlock, conciliation or war. There was much to be said for the former alternative, as will now appear.

It is a mistake to suppose that all Frenchmen and Alsatians longed for a war of revenge. Many of them realised the impossibility of such a scheme; and they also saw that, even if it succeeded, the holding of those provinces against a hostile Germany would impose crushing burdens upon France and perpetual unrest upon Europe[1]. Moreover, the teachings both of ethnology and history warned them against any such enterprise. The term Alsatia, once applied to a no-man's land in London, reminds us that Alsatia was in olden times a debateable land between Gaul and Teuton. In point of fact, the Alsatians are almost entirely German by race, and the ties of commerce connected her with the Teutons rather than the Gauls; for rivers connect peoples while mountains divide them. Consequently many influences

[1] See "*La Situation*" *par un Alsacien-Lorrain* (Geneva, 1887); Sir T. Barclay, pp. 312-4.

told against a complete absorption of Alsace into France[1]. Therefore they pleaded for the neutralisation of the annexed provinces. Arguments in favour of that solution were well set forth at the International Peace Congress held at Geneva in 1884. Several Frenchmen protested against that solution on the ground that the provinces wanted union with France. Others, however, notably M. Demolins, advocated the middle course. He pointed out that during 1000 years those districts had formed a debatable land between the French and German peoples, neither of which could hold them permanently. Therefore, was it not better to pronounce the struggle a draw? A recent book by Herr Maas of Leipzig, *Die Vereinigten Staaten Europas*, had urged the neutralisation of the provinces, all the fortresses being dismantled, "for the "strength of a nation consists in the ascendancy of "light, science, and law." Ardently endorsing these proposals, Demolins appealed to the Germans to give up their militarism, alike cramping to themselves and menacing to their neighbours. Frenchmen, on their side, must abandon all thought of a war of revenge, and be satisfied to see Alsace-Lorraine independent and neutral. This solution, however, by no means satisfied an Alsatian delegate, Waag of Colmar, who spoke passionately for union with France as the cherished desire of all Alsatians. Their civilization was Roman, not Germanic[2]. The final vote of the Conference showed a perplexing balance between the cosmopolitan and the national solutions. Twelve of the delegates voted for neutralising Alsace-Lorraine, six opposed it, six abstained

[1] See, too, M. Leroy, ch. I.
[2] So E. Hinzelin, p. 153.

from voting, and one resigned. Nothing could better
indicate the difficulty of the question. The only topic
on which there was an approach to unanimity was in
regard to the preliminary step, that Alsace-Lorraine
must be allowed to express freely by a mass-vote their
desires for their future.

Any such proposal was vetoed by the German Government; and the outlook, as we have seen, became more
gloomy under William II. Then the spirit of Treitschke
began to prevail in Germany. In 1871 the professor
had raged at the lenient terms accorded to France; and
the burden of his professorial message was that Germany,
now strong in herself, must expand by force of arms:
" War is the mightiest and most efficient moulder of
" nations. Only in war does a nation become a nation,
" and the expansion of existing States proceeds in most
" cases by way of conquest." As for the notion of
seeking the consent of the annexed people, he ridicules
it: " States do not arise out of the people's sovereignty,
" but they are created against the will of the people[1]."
Doubtless, he deduced this principle from the war of
1866, which created the North German Confederation
despite the opposition of the Prussian Parliament. But,
with the *perfervidum ingenium Prussorum*, he expanded
that single instance into a universal truth. Monstrous!
you will say. True; but the youth of Germany believe
it. Hence the soul of Germany became hardened against
the appeals of pity that came from the Reichsland.
And when the Pan-German idea came to reinforce professorial fallacies, all hope of a compromise respecting
Alsace-Lorraine vanished.

[1] Treitschke, *Die Politik*, Bk. i. § 4.

Yet, if the Pan-Germans had been logical, they would have allowed some discussion on the subject of Metz. That city was thoroughly French, as were all the villages around; so too was Thionville. For this reason, Bismarck, as we have seen, secretly disapproved the annexation of Metz and its environs. Further, on historical grounds Germany had no right to Metz; for though that city had been connected with the Holy Roman Empire, yet the link was very slight[1]. Besides, language was an insuperable barrier. There is, I believe, no example in history of a French-speaking people giving up their mother-tongue and taking to German, though instances to the contrary might be cited. Consequently, the Germanising of Metz was hopeless. On the occasion of State visits numbers of people could be drafted in to cheer the Emperor[2]; but the cheers of these hired *claqueurs* were openly ridiculed.

Accordingly, some Germans came to see the desirability of exchanging Metz for some French colony, an exchange which might have eased the tension. The colonial party in Germany would have scored a success, and France would no longer have fumed at seeing French-speaking people at her very doors dragooned by Germans. Further, she would have been free from that military menace, the great bastion of Metz thrust forth into the levels of Lorraine. In every respect the crux of the Franco-German problem is at Metz. The Kaiser, however, and the leaders of German opinion scouted all thought of an exchange which would restore that city

---

[1] Dom Calmet, *Hist. ecclésiastique et civile de la Lorraine*, II. p. 1296; H. Maringer, *Force au Droit*, pp. 65–83.

[2] *Mems. of Prince Hohenlohe*, II. p. 350 (Engl. edit.).

to France. This appears even in a little book, *England and Germany*, published in 1912. It consists of a number of articles urging friendlier relations between the two countries. Sir Thomas Barclay, whose labours helped on the Anglo-French Entente, pointed out that that measure was not hostile to Germany; but that our friendship to France caused us to take a lively interest in the Alsace-Lorraine Question, which held Germany and France apart; and he suggested that the statesmen of Berlin should approach those of Paris with a view to finding some *modus vivendi*. The response from the German contributors was disappointing. Baron von Pechmann, a Munich banker, reprobated any discussion of the Treaty of Frankfurt of 1871, which assigned Alsace-Lorraine to the Fatherland. Ignoring the fact that Metz stood in a very different relation from Strassburg to the German Empire, he asserted that the possession of the whole of the annexed districts was an absolute necessity to Germany : " Anyone who questions that right " is guilty of a wrong to Germany, a wrong that hurts " us in a very sensitive spot, one which not only calls " in question our rights but the most sacred memories " in our history and everywhere in the world the inalien-" able and inviolable quality of our national honour." These are the words, not of a Prussian bureaucrat, but of a South German banker; and they are uttered in rejection of a friendly suggestion, that Germany should approach France with a view to some compromise respecting Alsace-Lorraine. If that is the spirit of all Germans, war with France, was, I admit, inevitable. I do not believe, however, that all Germans would have excluded from discussion the French part of Lothringen.

Many of them desired a compromise. But so long as Treitschke swayed the convictions, and the Kaiser excited the emotions, of the German nation, a friendly settlement, even as regards Metz, was out of the question.

For the spirit in which a nation approaches a political problem is more important even than the problem itself. Who would have said, early in 1904, that the many causes of dispute between Great Britain and France would be amicably settled in that year? During two centuries and more the two peoples had been quarrelling about the fish off Newfoundland. For a couple of decades they had been snarling about Egypt, Madagascar, the Niger, and Siam. And then, thanks to the tact of King Edward VII and Lord Lansdowne, they speedily discovered that cod-fish and fellaheen, Malagasy, Haussas, and Siamese, were not worth a war. But that discovery came about because on both sides of the Channel there existed a latent longing for peace, which, with fostering care, could become vocal and speedily drown or resolve the earlier discords.

But how did Germany regard the Anglo-French entente? As a lesson in the methods by which disputes may be solved peaceably? She might have viewed it in that light; and there are good grounds for believing that we should have gone far to meet her. Lord Rosebery in his speech of October 25, 1905, stated emphatically that our understanding with France ought not to be regarded as a threat to Germany, but, on the contrary, that we desired friendlier relations with her. Still more important is Lord Lansdowne's letter of May 8, 1904, to Sir Thomas Barclay. He expressed his desire " to see all matters which might give rise to controversy

" between ourselves and other countries happily settled[1]."
If that was the spirit animating our Foreign Minister,
we may be sure that he endeavoured to include Germany
within the scope of the recent cordial understanding
with France. Further, it is contrary to all that is known
of the convictions of his successor, Sir Edward Grey,
to suppose that he too would not have welcomed such
an arrangement.

But was Germany disposed to meet us half-way?
The Pan-German writer, Count Reventlow, supplies the
answer. Discussing the proposals that passed between
London and Berlin on that question, he declares that
they were not feasible; for a British alliance would in
the future have tied Germany's hands. The ally would
inevitably ask Germany to consent to a proportional
diminution of the British and German naval programmes
as a sign of trust and goodwill. Germany, however,
could not lessen her naval preparations. She must keep
a free hand to build warships as she saw fit, otherwise
she would be in a worse position relatively to Great
Britain. Equally must she be free to pursue her World-
Policy[2]. These admissions are illuminating. They show
the reason why the proposal of an Anglo-German-Japanese
entente in 1901 came to nought, also the causes of the
failure of King Edward and his statesmen to include
Germany in the entente cordiale with France. The
latter failure is easily intelligible, despite the efforts of
Frenchmen (e.g. M. Jules Lemaître). It is summed up
in the words, Alsace-Lorraine[3].

---

[1] Sir T. Barclay, p. 312.   [2] Reventlow, pp. 178–9.
[3] M. Leroy, chs. IV, V; V. M. Laurent, etc. *Le Paix armée et le
Problème d'Alsace* (1914).

Even so, the statesmen of Berlin should not have interpreted that entente as a threat to them, but rather as a sign of affability to France. But they could not, or would not, see. They interpreted every act of Great Britain in the most unfavourable sense[1]. An English princess could not marry a Continental prince without cries being raised all over the Fatherland that we were hemming it in by alliances; though, surely, we were not to blame if neither the supply was so bounteous nor the demand so keen in regard to German princesses. These acrid complaints were signs of a mental disease which it is difficult to diagnose apart from the teachings of Treitschke and Bernhardi. Its most prominent symptom was an unreasoning Chauvinism, which, after the military collapse of Russia in Manchuria, took the form of intolerable arrogance both towards France in Moroccan affairs and towards Russia in those of the Balkan Peninsula.

[1] *e.g.*, Reventlow, *passim.*

LECTURE VI

THE EASTERN QUESTION

When the Balkan States form a compact body, opposing firm resistance to every attempt upon their union, all covetousness will cease, and the East will no longer be a menace to the peace of Europe.
Signor Tittoni, Speech in the Chamber at Rome, Dec. 3, 1908.

The Serbs of Bosnia-Herzegovina have twice set Europe in a blaze—in 1875 when their revolt against Turkish misrule reopened the Eastern Question, and again in June, 1914, when two of their fanatics murdered the Austrian Archduke, Francis Ferdinand. These two events remind us of the diverse issues that confronted the Christian peoples of the Balkans in the past generation and in our own day. In 1875 the Turk was the one and only enemy. In 1914 the enemy is Austria. Thus, there has come about an almost bewildering change over the problem known as the Eastern Question. But, before we seek to gauge the importance of that change and of its present issues, let us try to understand the essentials of that Question.

It is a profoundly national problem, the most complex which has distracted the world since the break up of the Roman Empire. The feuds of hostile races and creeds in the Balkan Peninsula have been keener than in any other part of Europe; and this is due, firstly, to geographical causes. Peninsulas are like pockets hanging from the mainland. They hold up the flotsam and jetsam of humanity. Wales, Brittany, the Iberian Peninsula, Italy, all are examples of the working of this ethnic law. But the Balkan Peninsula, gaping widely towards the North, has collected far more peoples than any other peninsula except India. It has gathered in the races wandering from East to West, who were deflected southwards by the great barrier of the Carpathians. It also held up the reflux from the North-West and wedged it against the far greater drift from the North-East.

But the Balkan Peninsula is not only a great wallet, it is also (if I may violently change the metaphor) a bridge, the easiest way from Asia into Europe. As such it brought the Turks into Europe. Nearly a century before their capture of Constantinople (1453) they harried the Balkan lands. In 1389 they utterly crushed the Serbs in the Battle of Kossovo, which that brave little people yearly laments. Their grief is natural; for that disaster ended their days of splendour. It is Kossovo, not the capture of Constantinople, which marks the beginning of the Eastern Question. Thereafter the Turks overcame the Bulgars, a warlike race of Tartar origin who became Slavised and Christianised after their settlement in the Balkan Peninsula. The crescent also prevailed over the Greeks and Roumans. Thus there began that long agony, the subjection of brave and civilized Christian peoples to a Tartar horde which could neither understand, assimilate, nor even govern them. During ages the Osmanli Turks, the bravest but most ignorant and fanatical of the Moslem peoples, studied practically nothing but the Koran, a bewildering jumble of precepts calculated to muddle the clearest of brains. Napoleon greatly admired the Koran because it made men good fighters. Yes; but if its votaries were wolves in war, they were sheep in time of peace, especially before the head shearer, the Sultan. Valiant in fight, but helpless in the art of government, they slowly yielded ground before their Christian subjects, until in our own day the strife in the Balkans became balanced. It was reserved for the little peoples of the Balkans in the *épopée* of 1912 (surely worthy of a second Tchaikovsky) to defy with success the western Moslems, who in the middle ages had beaten back the forces of the whole of Christendom.

In those long struggles for liberation, ranging over nearly 250 years, two external States have played a helpful part, Russia and Austria. But here we must distinguish between the motives that prompted intervention by those Powers. The Russian people has always taken keen interest in the struggles of Serb and Bulgar against the Sublime Porte. Kinship in race and community of religion (that of the Greek Church) impelled them to intervene. The generous feelings that led mankind to undertake the Crusades have nerved the Muscovites in their wars against the Turks. True, ambition has often prompted the policy of their Government, from the times of Peter the Great and Catherine II onwards; but the rank and file have been actuated by a noble impulse, the desire to free the oppressed and to plant the cross once more on the dome of St Sophia at Constantinople. This is the feeling which nerved the soldiers of Suvorof and Diebitsch to their deeds of heroism. It is the same feeling, largely,

which inspires them now to overthrow the last but
deadliest enemy of the Balkan Slavs, Austria.

During more than a century the House of Hapsburg
has had no similar motive for intervention in Balkan
affairs.   But, as the Ottoman power decayed, the Statesmen of Vienna discerned in the south-east the line of
least resistance for their imperial projects.   Italian
patriots, notably Count Balbo, urged the Hapsburgs to
turn towards the Balkans the energies which were vainly
employed beyond the Alps to hold down Italians[1].   His
prophecy in 1843 was fulfilled in 1866, when Austria was
expelled both from Italy and from the Germanic confederation.   After the formation of the German Empire under
the headship of Prussia, the polyglot Hapsburg dominions
could expand only towards the Balkans.   Hence the
principle of growth which pushes the Germans towards
the North Sea and into new lands, also urges Austria
towards the Ægean.   We must recognise that in both
cases an impulse natural to a vigorous people is driving
on these movements.   In the interests of the little
peoples who are threatened on the lower Rhine and
Meuse, as well as on the lower Danube, we must oppose
such forcible expansion; but it has in it something of
the elemental, which, in the wiser future that is surely
ahead, will demand satisfaction by methods less brutal
than war.

In this brief study of the Eastern Question we must
limit ourselves mainly to the ever increasing rivalry
between Austria and the Balkan Slavs and their champion,
Russia.   In the years 1875–7 that rivalry was restrained
by the counsels of prudence which then prevailed in

[1] C. Balbo, *Le Speranze d' Italia* (Turin, 1843).

presence of the rising power of democracy. The three Empires, still loosely connected by the Three Emperors' League, sought to localize the Herzegovinian Rising and to induce Turkey to grant the needed reforms. We now see that pacific coercion of the Sublime Porte was the sole method for ending the troubles in the North-West of its Empire; and it is generally agreed that the support offered by the British Government to the Turks was a political blunder of the first magnitude. At once they stiffened their necks; and the new Sultan Abdul Hamid II, prepared to defy Russia if she took up the cause of the now despairing Christians of the Balkans.

Mark what ensued. Britain's policy having broken up the Concert of the Powers which had sought to end the crisis peaceably, the former rivals, Russia and Austria, came to a secret agreement. Regarding war between Russia and Turkey as inevitable, they agreed to the following compromise. Austria would remain neutral, provided that Russia respected the integrity of Roumania, and did not annex land south of the Danube. It was also understood that she should confine her military operations to the eastern half of the Peninsula. Austria, however, exacted a high price for her neutrality, viz. the occupation of Bosnia at the end of the war. But this by no means satisfied the statesmen of Vienna. The severe defeats sustained by Russia before Plevna whetted their appetite for Balkan lands; and in the spring of 1878, before the Berlin Congress which was to settle the Eastern Question, they demanded that Austria should occupy the whole of Albania and Macedonia, including Salonica. Bosnia was also to become a principality dependent on the Hapsburgs; and Austria was to acquire

the right to make special treaties with Serbia and Montenegro, on terms which would have made them virtually
dependent on her[1].

She did not gain these concessions.　But she procured
the insertion in the Treaty of Berlin of Articles 25 and 29,
which empowered her provisionally to occupy the Sanjak
of Novi Bazar, and also to extend her influence beoynd
Mitrovitza, its southernmost limit.　This was equivalent
to handing her the key to Macedonia and bidding her
advance to Salonica when she saw fit; and on several
occasions she seemed about to begin the march to Salonica,
to which the chauvinists of Vienna constantly impelled
her[2].

The Balkan peoples lived in perpetual dread of such
an event.　Mr Minchin found during his sojourn in
Bosnia and Serbia that the Montenegrins dreaded Austria
far more than their ancient foes, the Turks.　So did the
Greeks.　The Turk was in his dotage, but his place
would at once be taken by the active and intriguing
Austrian, and then farewell to all hopes of a Greek
Salonica[3].　Most of all, the Serbs dreaded Hapsburg
aggression.　True, Austria coquetted with King Milan,
but only on condition that he worked in her interests.
In 1885 she also saved the Serbs from the advance of
the victorious Bulgars; but she could do no less; for she
had incited them to attack the Bulgars; and when her
protégés were badly beaten she of course intervened; but
thereafter she was described as the shadow hanging over

[1] Débidour, *Hist. diplomatique de l'Europe*, II. 515.

[2] Tittoni, *Italy's Foreign and Colonial Policy* (Eng. edit.), pp. 139–
143.

[3] J. Minchin, *Growth of Freedom in the Balkan Pensinula*, pp. 19,
32, 221; Cassavetti, *Hellas and the Balkan Wars*, p. 226,

the whole of Serbia. Indeed, it would seem that nothing
but the dread of increasing the Slav population of the
Dual-Monarchy prevented its statesmen from annexing
Serbia outright. There were credible reports that both
King Milan and afterwards King Alexander were about
to place Serbia under vassalage to Austria.

The Albanians were equally apprehensive. Both
Austria and Italy coveted their land, especially its coast
line, which commands the entrance to the Adriatic.
Those nominal Allies could scarcely forbear laying violent
hands on that important coast, a question which in the
winter of 1912–3 nearly brought about a European War.

We must now trace the growing rivalry between Austria
and Russia in Balkan affairs. Early in the present
century Austria began to gain ground far more quickly
than Russia in Balkan Questions. This may be explained
by her advantages of position, her skill in the management
of half-civilized races, and the firm backing of Germany.
The support of Berlin is intelligible in the light of events
described in Lecture IV. So as soon the Bagdad Railway
scheme took definite form, in the year 1902, Germany
had every reason for desiring Austria to control the
Balkan lands, and therefore the through railway lines
from Central Europe to Constantinople. These schemes,
linked as they were with the Bagdad and Hedjaz Railways
were so vast that the Sultan ought to have perceived
their menacing character. But Germany convinced him
of her goodwill—England had stolen Egypt and Cyprus;
France had annexed Tunis; Italy coveted Tripoli;
Russia threatened Armenia. The Austrians might be
dangerous in Macedonia; but Germany would see that
they did the Turk no harm; and by her railways she

sought to do Turkey nothing but good. The Germans, in fact, were the only sincere friends that Turkey had in the world[1]. Moreover, the Kaiser encouraged the Sultan to persevere in the Pan-Islam movement. In fact, Pan-Germanism and Pan-Islamism acting together would stalemate Pan-Slavism. The crafty Sultan was completely cajoled; and during many years Berlin virtually swayed the counsels of the Sublime Porte, giving it *carte blanche* in regard to the Christians of Macedonia and Armenia. The more the British Government and Press protested against his policy of terrorism and massacre, the more he leant on the Kaiser; and a large share of the responsibility for those horrors must fall to the imperial moralist and preacher of Potsdam. For the time his pro-Turkish policy succeeded. The influence of Berlin superseded that of Great Britain and France; and it promised to support Turkey even against the dreaded Muscovite.

Thus, the Teutonic programme was as follows: Germany would partly support, partly control Turkey (meanwhile exploiting Asia Minor) while Austria was to become supreme in Serbia, Bulgaria, and finally in Macedonia. That accomplished, the Germanic Empires might hope for the Empire of the Orient.

How came Russia to permit these schemes? We must here remember that Russia in 1900 successfully opposed the northern route of the Bagdad Railway; and, having diverted the line far from her Caucasian borders, she now viewed the scheme with less reluctance, especially as it promised to link up her Persian lines with the Bagdad system. Russia, moreover, at that time was chiefly intent on her Trans-Siberian railway schemes

[1] Reventlow, p. 313.

and the construction of great naval and commercial bases on the Pacific at Port Arthur and Dalny. The Far East diverted her from the Near East. The statesmen of Petrograd and of Tokio are said to be convinced that Germany lured Russia on to the dangerous schemes in Korea which embroiled her with Japan, an explanation which seems reasonable in view of the reconciliation between the two Powers, which came about speedily after the end of the war.

Certain it is that, some ten to fifteen years ago, Russia took far less interest in Balkan affairs than formerly. In 1903, when on the brink of the Japanese War, she came to terms with Austria in what was known as the Mürzsteg programme of reforms. Ostensibly it aimed at the improvement of the lot of the oppressed peoples of Macedonia under the joint supervision of Austria and Russia. That the two rivals should join hands in promoting philanthropic schemes caused cynics to sneer; and unfortunately the cynics were right. The scheme was supposed virtually to supplant the obligations laid upon all the Great Powers by the Treaty of Berlin. England, enfeebled by the Boer War, was glad to hand over her responsibilities as regards the Christians of Turkey. France and Italy took much the same view; while Germany was hand and glove with the Sultan, the sworn foe of all reforms. When Russia was defeated in the Far East, Austria virtually let the Mürzsteg programme lapse[1]. But in the meantime she had secured the first place in Balkan affairs.

Signs of her activity have been portrayed in the sprightly pages of Miss Edith Durham. She describes the splendour of the Austrian consulates then being built

[1] Reventlow, p. 316.

in Albania and Macedonia. She says, "The consul lives
"in a palace, and has a whole staff of lively youths,
"whose principal business in life appears to be taking
"holidays for shooting expeditions, and whose knowledge
"of the land is minute and exhaustive. They will even
"take you out for a walk and tell you the improvements
"which their Government means to introduce in a few
"years' time." She once asked one of them whether
a new consulate was not large enough for a Governor's
palace. He at once replied: "Then it will be very useful
"to us in a few years' time[1]."

The first great *coup* came in 1908. Austria then
annexed Bosnia-Herzegovina outright. The Powers protested vigorously, all the more so because the Young
Turks had just gained power at Constantinople amidst
the plaudits of an astonished world. But while visions
of a political millennium seemed to be taking shape on
the Bosphorus, there fell this heavy blow from Austria.
Was it her way of discrediting the new system, detested
by Germany, acclaimed by Great Britain? Or was it
merely a coincidence that the annexation came at the
time of the Diamond Jubilee of Francis Joseph, providing
him with a present of imperial splendour? Or, again,
was it that Russia was still weak and could not resent
Austria's expansion in the Balkans?

It is certain that the Austrian statesman who carried
through this stroke, had adopted a very different policy
from that usually associated with Vienna. During many
years Viennese policy had been conservative and cautious,
so that Austria had been called the House of Lords of
Europe. Up to the autumn of 1906 she was so passive

[1] E. Durham, *Burden of the Balkans*, ch. 3.

in foreign affairs that Kaiser William took occasion to describe her Foreign Minister, Count Goluchowski, as "a " brilliant second" during the Algeciras Conference of the spring of that year. Damned with faint praise, that Minister retired from office. His successor, Baron von Aehrenthal, soon proved to be a man after Kaiser William's own heart. He was enterprising, and thoroughly German. Above all he believed that the best means of stopping the eternal feuds in the Parliaments of the Dual Monarchy was to embark on a spirited foreign policy[1]:

> Be it thy course to busy giddy minds
> With foreign quarrels; that action, hence borne out,
> May waste the memory of the former days.

Those words, which Shakespeare puts in the mouth of Henry IV, as parting advice to his son, may stand as the motto of Austria's policy since 1906. Aehrenthal was only too ready to obey the impulses emanating from Berlin. He checked the pro-Slav tendencies in the Dual Monarchy and prepared to subject the Slavs on its southern borders. Russia, weakened by her disasters in Manchuria, was not likely to oppose him. As for Great Britain he openly flouted her; and he declined to take us seriously even after the conclusion of our entente with Russia in 1907. In fact in the autumn of that year he pushed on a railway scheme into Macedonia by way of Novi Bazar, and in order to procure the consent of the Porte he offered that Austria should renounce her participation in the Mürzsteg scheme of Macedonian reforms. His bargain with Turkey may be thus described: "You " Turks may do what you like in Macedonia if you will let " us build our railway." At home Aehrenthal defended his

---

[1] W. Steed, *The Hapsburg Monarchy*, pp. 224–230.

scheme on the ground that it would be an important link between Europe, Egypt, and India[1]. The mention of Egypt and India was, of course, meant as a threat to us.

These were the events preceding the annexation; and they explain the indignation which that event occasioned at Petrograd, Paris, and London. Austria, backed up by Germany, was clearly working to precipitate the ruin of the Turks by abandoning the reform programme which alone could save Macedonia from anarchy; but she was also pushing on a railway that would enable her to profit to the full by that anarchy. So soon as Turkey went to pieces, the white coats of Austria could be at the gates of Salonica. That was the way in which Vienna then regarded the Eastern Question; and it must be remembered that Germany, for all her bolstering up of the old Sultan's tyranny, was ready with railway schemes in Asia Minor so as to profit by the breakdown in Turkey which clear-sighted observers confidently predicted. She was prepared for either alternative, the continuance of Turkish tyranny, or the fall of the Sultan.

Why, then did she not push on her schemes when the Sultan's authority collapsed at the time of the Young Turks' triumph at Constantinople? Doubtless, because that event overthrew German influence at the Sublime Porte. It has even been asserted by German writers that the Young Turks dealt their stroke because just previously King Edward VII and the Tsar had met at Reval on the Gulf of Finland. *Post hoc ergo propter hoc.* Evidently (so argue these logicians) those potentates met for something. The Young Turk Revolution was some-

[1] W. Steed, *The Hapsburg Monarchy*, p. 235; Sir C. Eliot, *Turkey in Europe, ad fin.* (new edit. 1908); Reventlow, p. 316.

thing. Therefore the royal meeting met for the Young Turk Revolution. In the eyes of these writers King Edward was the Mephistopheles of the age, ever plotting the isolation of Germany.—His summer visits to Carlsbad or Ischl, where he often met Kaiser Franz Joseph, were intended to withdraw him from the German alliance, or tempt him to persuade Kaiser Wilhelm not to build ships so fast. And now at Reval King Edward and the Tsar launched the Young Turks against Abdul Hamid[1]. —It seems to us incredibly superficial. But very many Germans, judging other sovereigns by the phenomenal activity of their own, could not believe that anything great could happen unless some monarch or statesman contrived it.

Alas! The prospects of the reformers at Constantinople were speedily blighted by their follies and factions; and in April, 1909, there came to power a party favourable to Germany,—a result due largely to the skill of the German ambassador, Baron Marschall von Bieberstein. Since then she has resumed her former sway at Constantinople[2].

Meanwhile the two Germanic Empires had also won a diplomatic triumph. They made good their contention that Austria should annex Bosnia. The Triple Entente opposed them in vain. Russia was still weak; France knew that she would get no help from Petrograd, and took little interest in Balkan affairs. Great Britain took more interest; but, alone, she was helpless against the

---

[1] Reventlow, p. 322: the King and Tsar probably did not discuss politics (see W. Steed, p. 237).

[2] Sir W. Ramsay, *The Revolution in Constantinople and Turkey* (1909), pp. 15–17.

Triple Alliance. For at that time Italy held by her
Allies. True, she did so somewhat doubtfully; and her
Government was sharply criticized in the Chambers at
Rome for its pro-Austrian policy. But, by coming to an
understanding with Russia on Balkan affairs, the Cabinet
of Rome scored one success. At the Congress of the
Great Powers which deliberated on the Bosnian Question,
Austria had to consent to withdraw from the Sanjak of
Novi Bazar. She did so very reluctantly, and mainly, it
is said, owing to the insistence of Italy and Russia[1].

But mark the result of this withdrawal. It left only
one line of advance southwards to a Power which was
resolved to extend not only its railways but its political
power in the Balkans. This line was through Serbia,
which provided both the shortest and the easiest route
to Salonica. Indeed, a railway already ran right through
to the coveted port. Therefore the Austrian military
men and engineers consoled themselves with the thought
that thenceforth the route through Serbia must be the
object of Austria's efforts.

Serbia was exasperated by these events[2]. The annexation of Bosnia, and the handing back of the Sanjak to
the Porte shut her out from all hopes of reaching the
sea, which she had so long cherished. Through the 600
dark years which have rolled over her since the downfall
of her glorious kingdom, she had dreamed of once more
reaching the Adriatic. Now that dream was dispelled.
On all sides she felt herself threatened; for that most

---

[1] Tittoni, p. 142. For the Austro-Turkish bargain of February,
1909, which ended "the annexation crisis" (see W. Steed, p. 255).
Bülow, *Imperial Germany*, pp. 50–61.

[2] Reventlow, p. 328.

crafty of European rulers, Prince Ferdinand of Bulgaria, had recently taken a threatening step. Just before Austria's annexation of Bosnia, he had visited Vienna; and on his return proclaimed himself Tsar of the Bulgarians, a claim which implied sway over the million or more of Bulgars in Central and West Macedonia. This again seemed to blight Serbia's hopes of expanding southwards. Nay! She was threatened at her very heart by a war of tariffs with Austria. Her chief product was pigs; and now the Dual Monarchy refused to take them. The Turks refuse all pigs. Therefore the sole exit for Serb pigs was Bulgaria; but as the Bulgars had enough of their own, the future for the Serb animals became gloomy in the extreme. For a time King Peter and some of his counsellors are said to have thought of entering into some form of dependence on Austria at which that Empire had been aiming.

But, fortunately for the cause of the little States, they decided to fight, not each other, but rather the common enemy, either Turkey or Austria. One of their delegates to London in 1912, when questioned as to the date of their preparations for war, said that they were begun immediately after Austria's annexation of Bosnia; for all those peoples then felt their doom approaching[1].

The assertion may be commended to the German writers who have seen in the Balkan League merely the outcome of Russian intrigues. All who are acquainted with Balkan affairs know that it originated in a sense of despair of any reforms from the Young Turks or of effective help from the Great Powers. Germany and

---

[1] Letter of Mr Frederick St John in *Times*, August 14, 1914.

Austria blocked the way to intervention by the Great
Powers; and by the years 1911–12 the incredible folly
of the Young Turks led to hardships worse even than in
the days of Abdul Hamid. Only occasionally did he
order massacres. But the Young Turks persistently
pressed hard upon all the Christians of the Empire.
Trained at Paris or Berlin, they had imbibed the doctrine
that public affairs would go well if organized by a scientific
administration. To them nationality and religion were
absurd survivals, to be swept aside as soon as possible.
Turkey would prosper when her government resembled
that of Paris or Berlin. A sort of Pan-Turk propaganda
was set on foot to assimilate all the diverse peoples of the
empire. A Young Turk said to Miss Durham: "All is
"now simplified. The Greek, the Bulgar, the Serb, the
"Albanian Questions no longer exist. We have passed a
"law, and now all are Osmanli." To which Miss Durham
replied: "You can pass a law, if you like, that all cats
"are dogs; but they will remain cats."

In 1912 the opportunity for the little peoples had come.
In the previous autumn Turkey was attacked by Italy,
an event which disordered all the calculations of Berlin
and Vienna. It had long been known vaguely that
Italy desired Tripoli. So far back as 1878 Bismarck
had pointed her to that land, if France took Tunis.
But very few persons expected the blow to fall in
1911. Her part in the Triple Alliance was to act as a
passive third, behind Austria as a "brilliant second." On
one occasion Kaiser William said as much to an Italian
diplomat who complained of the lenten fare provided for
Italy by the Triple Alliance. He said to him: "Wait
"patiently. Let the occasion but present itself, and you

"shall have whatever you wish[1]." But Italy waited in vain. Her impatience became extreme in 1911; for by then France had cut a great slice out of Morocco, and Germany out of the French Congo. The Cabinet of Rome therefore resolved to strike at Tripoli; and those who watch the inner ironies of history will note with satisfaction that the Kaiser was hoist by Bismarck's petard, and that, too, at a time extremely inconvenient for the oriental designs of Germany. The railways were progressing favourably. The Turkish army and navy were said to be gathering strength. Even Turkish finances were said not to be hopeless. But now Italy spoilt the game.

As if this were not enough, the Turks chose this time of crisis for dragooning the Albanians and massacring Bulgars at Kochani in Macedonia. The Christian States therefore came to terms, framed their league, struck home; and within a month the Turkish Colossus lay prone.

But then came a terrible event. The victors fell out among themselves as to the share of Macedonia. The cause of these disputes is still obscure; but I have been informed by a diplomat of a Balkan State that it resulted largely from the vagueness of the original compact, which at first did not include Greece. Serbia and Bulgaria had arranged a general scheme for dividing Macedonia; but this proceeded on the assumption that Serbia would acquire Albania. She did acquire it by the prodigious exertions of her troops in the rush through snow and slush to Vallona. But it soon appeared that Austria and Italy would forcibly oppose her at that coast. Those two States very rarely pull together; but on this occasion they did, because each hoped to get Albania. Thus it came

---

[1] Crispi, *Mems.* III. 326 (Eng. edit.).

about that in the Congress of the Powers held in London
in 1912–13, Serbia had finally to give up North Albania.
It was a bitter blow to her people; but now they demanded
a larger share of Macedonia. To this the Bulgars demurred; and it is almost certain that their opposition in its
final stages was instigated by Austria. It is an open
secret that she encouraged her *protégé*, King Ferdinand,
to expect Austrian help if he rejected the demands of
Serbia. Several of the hotheads of Sofia hearkened to
this insidious advice. The Daneff Ministry at Sofia was
less to blame than has been generally believed. It was
pushed on to the brink of the precipice by the *chauvinists*.
Indeed, the final order to the Bulgarian troops to attack
the Serbs never had the signature of the responsible
Ministers. Insidious influences were certainly at work to
set the Christians of the Balkans by the ears; and those
influences emanated from Austria. She had resolved to
smash the Balkan League, whose victory over the Turks
had been a most unwelcome surprise. Both at Vienna
and Berlin it was believed that the Turks, drilled by
Germans, provided with Krupp's artillery, and rendered
doubly mobile by the new German railways in Asia Minor,
must prevail over allies who until lately had hated each
other more bitterly than the Turks. What wonder that
the Germanic Empires loathed the thought of a Turkey in
Europe controlled by four Christian States whose progressive culture marked out the future as theirs. The
German plans proceeded on the assumption that Turkey
would survive, at least long enough for the Teuton to
step in as residuary legatee. And now the Christian
States were about to share the best part of the inheritance.
Their triumph would imply the throwing in of four solid

blocks into the path which the Germanic Empires were resolved to control, the path leading from Berlin and Vienna to Constantinople and thence to the Persian Gulf.

In these considerations we may find the explanation of the miserable events of the summer of 1913, which exhausted the Balkan States and led to the conclusion of the unsatisfactory Peace of Bukharest, mainly at the dictation of the Germanic Powers. Here again they prevailed. They threw back the Slav cause in a way which caused keen satisfaction at Berlin and Vienna, but still keener resentment at Sofia, Belgrade, and Athens— above all at Petrograd. The Slavs had not sought this conflict, though this is constantly asserted at Berlin. It was forced on them by the aggressive designs of the two Germanic Empires, and, later, by the insane misgovernment of the Young Turks. Twice the Slav cause was set back by the action of Austria and Germany, viz. in the winters of 1908-9 and of 1912-13, on both of which occasions Europe narrowly escaped a general war. But the experience of those crises led to a firm resolve not to accept further humiliations from the Houses of Hapsburg and Hohenzollern.

LECTURE VII

THE CRISIS OF 1914

By whatever means we must be strong, so that by a powerful effort we may destroy our enemies in the east and in the west.

(German Secret Report, March 19, 1913.)

THE events in the Balkans during the year 1913 ushered in a time of severe tension. It was evident to all observers that the two Central Powers were bent on breaking up the Balkan League and securing their supremacy in that peninsula. The participation of beaten Turkey in that second war could scarcely have occurred without encouragement given from Berlin and Vienna. The intention evidently was to re-establish the Ottoman power as far as possible and deal a blow to the Slav cause both by lessening its gains of the year 1912 and by sowing discords among its champions. The plan met with startling success, and Austria might well hope finally to secure her supremacy in Turkey in Europe.

The secrets of those months are half revealed by some significant signs. Evidently the Sublime Porte must have considered itself very closely bound to the Central Powers; otherwise it would not now have intervened in this war. The Turkish troops are fighting with extreme reluctance; and it is well known that the Moslems of

India and Egypt regard Turkey's action as likely to lead to utter ruin. How close, then, must have been the grip which the German Powers fastened on Turkey in 1913! As to the Balkan States, though they nurse bitter hatred against each other, yet it is repressed by their over-mastering dread of Austria. Early in the present war it was expected that Bulgaria would attack Serbia in order to regain Central Macedonia. Why did she not do so? Because to do so would be to play the game for Austria; and her experience of the insidious policy of Vienna in 1913 has now kept her quiet.

Turn to Roumania. That State used to be on friendly terms with the Triple Alliance owing to re-sentment at the shabby conduct of Russia in 1878 in annexing Western Bessarabia. But her anger has abated. She no longer fears Russia; but she does fear Austria. On November 20, 1914, a leading Roumanian statesman, M. Jonescu, telegraphed to a Russian paper the following:—"All Roumania's interests "and her future are inseparably bound up with the "victory of the Triple Entente, to which Roumania must "contribute by participating in the war. Roumania "should strive to promote a Serbo-Bulgarian agreement "and do everything possible to come to terms with "Bulgaria, thus enabling all the Balkan States to side "with the nations of the Entente. A German victory "would mean the burial of all the hopes of the Balkan "States and of the independence of the neutral countries[1]." Roumania has her own special reasons for wishing the overthrow of Austria, from whom she hopes to recover the Roumans living north of the Carpathians. But she

[1] *Times*, Nov. 23, 1914.

also knows that Austrian supremacy in the Balkans would sound the death-knell of every free State in the Peninsula. Thus, the Aehrenthal policy has had the effect of uniting practically all the Balkan peoples against the menace from the north.

Hungary has behaved worse to the Slavs than Austria has done. In the Western half of the Monarchy a feeling not long ago prevailed in favour of encouraging the Slavs as a make-weight against the Magyars. In its extreme form this policy was known as *Trialismus*, *i.e.* a triple division of the Empire, the Slav provinces becoming a third division with Agram as capital. To the Magyars this notion spelt ruin, and they opposed it furiously. Thus, severe friction resulted, especially on the Serb border. There the Magyars sought to crush their Serb subjects, while these retaliated by a nationalist propaganda which sometimes led to fights and outrages. In the main, however, the Magyars carried things with a high hand, as was seen in that disgraceful episode, the Friedjung trial. For details I must refer you to the works of Messrs Seton-Watson and Wickham-Steed. Nowhere in Europe, except in Ireland, was there friction so acute as in the Slav provinces of Hungary; and it was there that friction first produced flame.

On June 28, 1914, two Bosnian Serbs murdered the heir to the throne of the Dual Monarchy, Archduke Franz Ferdinand. This dastardly crime aroused intense indignation against the Serbs. Their cowardly assassination of King Alexander and Queen Draga in 1903 was remembered; and all through Europe there rang denunciations of that "nation of assassins." There were suspicious features about the crime. The Archduke had favoured *Trialismus*; and the Archduchess was of Slav race. Therefore the murdered pair were more Slavonic in their sympathies than nine-tenths of those who now denounced the Serbs. But there can be no doubt as to the intense indignation which the crime at Serajevo aroused throughout the Austrian dominions; and it excited, what has been so rare in the recent history of that Empire, a passionate and general longing for war. A hackneyed saying of Napoleon assigns to moral power three-fourths of the might of an army. That moral power was now on the side of the " white-coats " about to wield the sword of justice against cowardly murderers. The Slav cause being disgraced, that of the Teuton bade fair to prevail. German and Magyar in the Dual Monarchy clasped hands enthusiastically;¯ and even their Slav subjects seemed likely to fight for good old Kaiser Franz against a nation that had put itself under the ban of Europe. The opportunity was all the more favourable because Austria generally viewed with suspicion and alarm the forward moves of Germany. As von Bernhardi said in the Preface to his book, *How Germany makes War*, neither Austria nor Italy took any interest in Germany's World-Policy. They were therefore certain to desert her if she began hostilities on her own account. But in July, 1914, Austria, the backward partner, was eager for war. What a chance! It might never again recur. Finally, there was this consideration, that the Tsar would probably be reluctant to draw the sword on behalf of "a nation of assassins." In the next lecture we shall see the use to which the Kaiser put this murder-motive.

Meanwhile notice that the war-party at Vienna began

forthwith to exploit the crime for their own ends, and to
plan forcible intervention in Serbia. The French ambassador in Vienna on July 2 reported as follows: "The
"inquiry into the origin of the outrage, which is to be
"demanded on conditions intolerable to the dignity of the
"Belgrade Government, would, in case of refusal, provide
"the excuse for proceeding to military execution." The
scheme was seen through at Petrograd. There the
Austrian ambassador stated that Austria might be forced
to search in Serbia for the accomplices of the crime.
Thereupon Sazonoff, Minister for Foreign Affairs, uttered
these warning words: "No country has suffered more
"than Russia from outrages planned upon foreign
"territory. Have we ever claimed to adopt against any
"country whatever the measures with which your news-
"papers threaten Serbia? Do not enter upon that path[1]."
Up to July 23 Austria delayed action. But the *Mili-
tärische Rundschau* clamoured for war.—"The moment is
"still favourable for us. If we do not decide upon war,
"the war we shall have to wage in two or three years at
"the latest will be begun in circumstances much less
"propitious. Now the initiative belongs to us. Russia
"is not ready; the moral factors are for us, might as well
"as right. Since some day we shall have to accept the
"struggle, let us provoke it at once." The *Neue Freie
Presse* demanded the extermination of the accursed
Serbian race[2].

    Let us now take a brief survey of the general situation
in Europe in the first seven months of 1914. In Russia
there was a very serious strike, which promised to paralyse

---

[1] French Yellow Book (1914), pp. 20, 21.
[2] *Ibid.* p. 22.

not only the tram service but also the transport service
of the Empire. Consequently that vast organism seemed
likely to move with far more than the traditional amount
of circumspection. Difficulties of mobilization have
always been great in Russia owing to the sparseness of
the population and the primitive nature of the means
of communication. Her railways are not all of the same
gauge; and the locomotives on different lines are constructed, some to burn wood, others coal or oil. But
strategic railways to her western frontier were either
planned or were in course of construction, an additional
motive why the Germans should act soon. Further,
in her three last wars, the Crimean, the Turkish, and the
Japanese, her organization had proved to be very defective.
Consequently, it was a proverb in historical circles that
Russia, however strong for defence (as against Charles XII
and Napoleon) was weak for offence; and in June, 1914,
her offensive power seemed at the lowest point. Russian
finances were also judged to be weak. In 1912 Dr Rohrbach stated that they would not bear the strain of a single
bad harvest. As for her army organization, it had been
improved somewhat since the Japanese War; but up to
1912 no real improvement had taken place. In an earlier
work he pronounced Russia's power to be overrated,
and he now repeated his verdict. Such, too, was the
report of the French diplomatic and consular agents in
Germany: "In political and military circles it is not
"believed that her assistance will be sufficiently rapid
"and energetic to be effective[1]."

Let us turn to France. In the spring and summer
of 1914 the French Republic was not in good odour.

[1] French Yellow Book (1914), p. 18.

The miserable Caillaux affair, with the resulting recrimi-
nations between Ministers of State, awakened a general
sense of distrust and alarm. Parliamentary Government
had long been on its trial, and now it seemed condemned.
Groups of men, struggling for power, displaced others so
soon as they were hopelessly discredited. Above them
there stood a manly figure, M. Poincaré, who typified
France; but he seemed powerless before the strife of the
factions. Worst of all, some Ministers stood accused
of selling State secrets to Germany. Then again, the
army was far from strong. True, the Chambers had in
the summer of 1913 passed a law reinforcing three years'
military service, a measure which promised to restore
the military efficiency latterly open to question. But
early in 1914 the supporters of the new Ministry threatened
to get that decree repealed. Everything therefore
became uncertain. Later on, on July 13, there took
place in the Chambers a debate, in which the army was
alleged to be ill equipped for war, boots and other
necessaries being deficient both in quality and quantity.
The disclosures sent thrills of alarm through France, of
exultation through Germany.

At that time, too, no small part of the French effectives
was still locked up in Morocco; and some weeks must
ensue before those war-hardened troops could form front
in Lorraine. Accordingly, Morocco was a drain on the
French army almost as serious as Mexico was to Napoleon
III in the crisis of 1866. German generals are known to
have rejoiced at the ending of the Agadir affair, which
gave France *carte blanche* in Morocco, because "it put
an elephant on the back of France." There was another
reason why they should act soon against France. When

she had thoroughly conquered Morocco, she could marshal an army corps of Moors, some of the bravest fighters in the world. For the present, Morocco held some 80,000 of her best troops. As for the French navy, once the second in the world, it had now sunk to fifth place.

The most serious feature in the life of France remains to be noted, the declining birth-rate. If that decline continued, France would obviously become a Power of the second rank. A German official puts it thus: "The "French may arm as much as they like. They cannot "from one day to another increase their population[1]." Count Reventlow urges that fact as a reason why King Edward chose to ally himself with France. She was a decadent nation, and therefore it was better policy to act along with her rather than with ever increasing Germany[2]. The argument is true if we assume that Great Britain desires to maintain the Balance of Power. But the argument is fatal to the Count's favourite thesis, the ceaseless greed of the islanders. If they were ever eager to clutch at a World-Empire, why did they not unite with powerful Germany to partition rich but decadent France and her extensive colonial empire? That we clasped the hand of the weaker State is a convincing refutation of the charges of selfish cunning so often flung at us.

What of the British Empire? In the year 1914 how did it stand in the eyes of the militant party of Berlin? Certainly there was much to excite their hopes. The Pan-Germans had long filled their books and journals with disquisitions on the inherent weakness of the British

[1] French Yellow Book (1914), p. 9.
[2] Reventlow, p. 233.

dominions. The arguments were curiously like those used by the French Republicans in 1793, adopted by Bonaparte, and then pressed home in his Continental System. An essay might be written on the theme *Delenda est Carthago*, as applied to England. The idea has captivated many a thinker, from the time of Quesnay and the French *Économistes* down to the German Agrarians of to-day. The fundamental notion is the same. Land is the basis of a State, and agriculture is the true source of wealth. Manufactures and commerce are later and artificial developments. The British, while relying on them, have neglected the source of real wealth, agriculture. Therefore England resembles a ship, light in ballast and with a fine show of top-hamper, destined to founder in the first tempest. The France of Napoleon I and the Germany of William II are well trimmed craft and will ride out the storm. Such is the theory. It is highly attractive, especially to the German Agrarians, as it enables them to tax foreign corn and thereby steady the ship of State and fill their own pockets.

One must admit that in the light of the teachings of history—Tyre, Carthage, Venice, Portugal, Holland—the persistent survival of Great Britain is the most exasperating of facts to theory-ridden professors; and this it is which, in part at least, accounts for our extreme unpopularity in German academic circles. That all the learning and ingenuity of the Fatherland should hitherto have stumbled over our rock of offence is an unpardonable crime. Treitschke, Rohrbach, Reventlow, Frobenius and others have proved to demonstration the fragility of the British Empire. It was won by guile. We set all the Continental States fighting and then stole the best lands

across the seas. The moral was obvious. Let all the
aggrieved States combine and compel the footpad to
disgorge. If the Pan-Germans had been wise, they
would have limited themselves to that programme, at
once moral and lucrative. For the British nation (they
said) was weak and degenerate, utterly given over to
sport, neglecting the first duty of citizenship by hiring
"mercenaries" to fight, detested by the Irish, and loathed
both by the Boers and the peoples of India. The landing
of a European force in South Africa (so said Rohrbach
in 1912) would lead to a rising of the Dutch population,
and that wealthy land would soon be lost to the Union
Jack. In that year Germany made formidable military
preparations in South-West Africa. As will be seen in
the Appendix, ammunition and stores sufficient to equip
a force of 10,000 men for six years were in that colony
in the autumn of 1912; and about that number of men
were ready to take the field. German officials, when
questioned, said that these preparations were against the
Ovambos in the north; but that native tribe was absolutely
quiet; and the chief preparations were in the south, not
far from the border of Cape Colony. Finally it became
known through an intercepted letter to the German
cruiser *Eber*, at Cape Town, that orders were issued at
Berlin, *on June* 14, 1914, whereby that ship and others
would be supplied with coal by means therein described,
if war ensued[1].

Reverting to Rohrbach, we note his estimate of the
defensive power of Australia. He declared that she
could not resist if her four chief towns, all of them near
the coast, were occupied by an invader. As for Canada,

[1] *Times*, Oct. 6, 1914.

she was sparsely peopled and had no military force worthy
of mention. India was discontented; the handful of
white administrators did not understand the people,
who were always on the brink of revolt. The appearance
of a single Russian army-corps on the Indus would lead
to the collapse of British rule. Egypt, the keystone of
the imperial arch, could easily be dislodged by the Moslems
in a Holy War. Above all the heart of the Empire was
weak; for the British people were too enervated by
luxury and selfishness to cope with the difficulties presented
by their overgrown Empire[1]. The hopes which Germany
placed in a general rising of Moslems against Great
Britain, Russia and France, are strikingly shown in a
German secret report, dated Berlin, March 19, 1913,
which advocated extensive preparations for war. It
proceeded thus: "Disturbances must be stirred up in
"Northern Africa and in Russia. This is a means of
"absorbing the forces of the adversary. It is, therefore,
"vitally necessary that through well-chosen agents we
"should get into contact with influential people in Egypt,
"Tunis, Algiers and Morocco, in order to prepare the
"necessary measures in case of a European war. These
"secret allies would, of course, be recognized openly in
"time of war....They should have a guiding head, who
"might be found among influential religious or political
"chiefs. The Egyptian school is specially suited for
"this. More and more it gathers together the intellectuals
"of the Moslem world[2]."

Even those who did not depreciate Great Britain to

---

[1] Rohrbach, *Deutschland unter den Welt-Völkern* (1908), pp. 67–164;
Der deutsche Gedanke in der Welt (1912), pp. 168–176.

[2] French Yellow Book (1914), pp. 9, 10.

this extent, proclaimed the need of beating her down.
General von Bernhardi in his second book, *Unsere Zukunft*
(Berlin, 1912), declared that a naval war with her might
be successful; she found great difficulty in manning her
fleet by the voluntary system; and (said he), "she seems
"to be approaching the limits of her naval capacity. In
"the second place the Baltic and North Sea Canal will
"soon be finished, and its completion will yield consider-
"able military advantages to Germany. Lastly, the
"German navy grows from year to year, so that the
"conclusion lies near, that the comparative strength of
"the two navies will gradually be altered to England's
"disadvantage. In the Mediterranean the Austrian and
"Italian navies are about to be strengthened." He then
says it is clearly to the interest of Great Britain to provoke
a war with Germany as soon as possible. This advice
to us (we may notice) was a counterpart to that which
in 1911 he had given to Germany in his work, now
translated,—*Germany and the next War*. At the end of
that book he spoke thus: "Even English attempts at a
"rapprochement [to Germany] must not blind us to the
"real situation. We may at most use them to delay the
"necessary and inevitable war until we may fairly imagine
"we have some prospect of success."

Those prospects of success mounted high in the
summer of 1914. Firstly, because Germany at Midsummer
opened the enlarged Kiel Canal. In consequence of the
general adoption of the *Dreadnought* type of battleship
she had been forced in 1905 to set about the widening and
deepening of that canal, so as to admit the passage of
her new warships, the first of which was launched in
1908 and completed (I believe) by 1911. Other ships of

the *Dreadnought* type soon followed. But none of them could pass quickly from the Baltic to the North Sea or *vice versâ* until that canal was widened and deepened, as it was at an estimated cost of £12,000,000. The completion was fixed for 1915, a time when Germany expected to have 18 *Dreadnoughts* or *Super-Dreadnoughts* ready, or nearly ready, for sea. By great exertions and additional expense she completed the canal at Midsummer, 1914. She had every reason for haste. In 1910 she transferred her large battleships from Kiel to Wilhelmshafen: and, until the canal was completed, they would be unable quickly to reach the Baltic and confront the Russian fleet. After 1914 Germany could expect to overpower in succession both the Russian and French navies if they came out of port. She held the interior position between them, an immense advantage at all times; and that advantage was now enhanced by the means of swift entry either into the Baltic or North Sea.

These considerations are all important for a due understanding of the course of German policy. It is a policy based on military and naval considerations. In 1866 she forced on a war with the Hapsburg Power because she had the needle-gun, while other circumstances also promised success to her arms. The same holds good of the war of 1870. Indeed, writers who neglect the military and naval situation leave out of count the determining factor of the policy of Berlin. Germany has enjoyed an astonishing series of triumphs because she does not go to war for an idea or a principle, but because she awaits a time favourable for dealing a sudden blow. That is the essence of *Realpolitik*. Even when she does not deal the blow, her diplomacy is coloured by the military and naval situation. Note the following facts. Her tone became far more aggressive in the year 1895, the year in which the Kiel Canal was first opened. She then adopted a high tone towards us in the Congo and South African Questions, the latter of which nearly led to war. The spurt thereby given to British naval construction served to impose respect upon her during the Boer War; but she then began to build very fast. The Ententes with France and Russia and increased naval construction were our methods of retort. She, too, pushed on her navy as fast as possible; but the adoption of the *Dreadnought* placed her for a time at a great disadvantage, because, after the completion of her first *Dreadnoughts* in 1911–12, she could not send them through her ship-canal; and in view of the persistence of the Anglo-Russo-French entente, which she found to be solid at the time of the Bosnian crisis of 1908–9, she had to prepare to face a naval war with all three Powers. She then made greater efforts than ever, and so did her Allies, Austria and Italy. By the Naval Act of 1912 she provided that about four-fifths of her marine should always be kept on a war footing; and so threatening was the situation which thus came about that the British Admiralty for a time decided to leave the Mediterranean, a resolve which emphasized our reliance on France in that quarter. It was clear, then, that Germany was beginning to run us close. Still, she could not well face a war until the great strategic advantages of the Kiel Canal were again at her disposal. Therefore, on naval grounds it was desirable for her to postpone a war until after the completion of that great work. This fact was well understood in naval circles. In 1913 Commandant Davin of the French navy wrote

an article reviewing the naval resources of Germany and
pointing out that the Canal changed a weak naval base
into a very strong one. He therefore concluded that
she would await the completion of that work before
declaring war[1].

But why did she hurry on the Canal so as to be ready
by Midsummer, 1914? Here the state of the French
and Belgian armies must be considered. The efficiency
of the French army was certain soon to increase owing
to the operation of the law of 1913, reinforcing three years'
military service. The Belgian army also was becoming
stronger every year. In 1910 that Government carried
a law imposing compulsory service for one son at least
in every family. But in 1912, owing to alarming advice
respecting German plans, the Chambers at Brussels
extended the principle of compulsory service with few
exceptions to males physically fit, above the age of
nineteen. This would bring to the colours as many as
56,000 men in 1914–15, instead of 35,000, the contingent
for 1912–13. Inclusive of the militia reserve, the grand
total would amount to 200,000 men at the end of 1913.
Finally it would rise to 340,000. It is certain that Germany took into consideration this increase.

The new Army and Taxation Bills introduced into
the Reichstag on April 7, 1913, led to an interesting
discussion, the Imperial Chancellor stating that it was the
duty of the Government to train 60,000 men more every
year, in order to meet the proposed increases of the
French and Russian armies. He also pointed out the
difficulty of acceding to Mr Churchill's proposal of a

[1] *La Revue des Questions diplomatiques* (1913), pp. 417, 418.

Naval Holiday. The Minister for War then stated that the object of the Bills was to render possible an offensive strategy if war came; for "the best parry is the lunge: "the best covering force is the offensive." The new taxation comprised a drastically graduated Property Tax, as well as Death Duties and Increment Duties, against which the Conservatives protested. The Imperial Budget subsequently empowered a special vote for expenditure of £21,000,000; but that sum has been largely exceeded. It is known that the purchase of petrol in 1914 was double, and of corn nearly double, of that in average years. The opinion became prevalent that this drastic taxation could not last; and a feeling of restlessness increased. German newspapers stated that £40,000,000 would be spent on war material by July 1.

A rupture of the peace of Europe appeared so imminent on the Albanian-Montenegrin disputes as to justify the Powers in taking financial precautions. Those of Germany were especially thorough, probably because her credit suffered severely at the time of the Agadir crisis in 1911. The wholesale collapse which was then barely averted led her to take measures to avert a crash in the event of war. The full details of her action with the Banks are not known. But the German Secret Report of March 19, 1913, laid down these guiding principles—There must be a great increase in armaments and consequently in taxation, so that "an outbreak [of war] shall be considered "as a deliverance, because after it would come decades "of peace and prosperity, such as those which followed "1870. The war must be prepared for from a financial "point of view. There is much to be done in this direction. "The distrust of our financiers must not be aroused, "but, nevertheless, there are many things which it will "be impossible to hide[1]."

Accordingly, on July 3, 1913, amidst a time of great prosperity, a law was passed authorising the addition of gold and silver equal in value to £12,000,000[2]. This sum was to be added to the imperial reserve of £6,000,000 deposited in 1871 in the fortress of Spandau. In addition, there was in the Banks of Issue bullion of the value of £86,960,000. Thus, the total value of gold and silver reserve was £104,960,000. But the Government was also ready with measures calculated to meet a sudden demand for money. On August 1, 1914, it suspended cash payments at the Banks and issued a large amount of paper notes and silver coins. The imperial reserve was also made available, and the Government immediately established banks for the issue of loans even for very small amounts on the security of goods and securities of all kinds, thereby becoming a paternal pawnbroker. There was therefore no need of a moratorium, and Germany prided herself on the ease with which she adapted herself to a state of war.

All had been thought out beforehand; and there was little confusion, certainly far less than was the case here. The British Government had no plans ready for meeting the financial strain; and at the close of July we were face to face with a very serious situation. The Joint Stock Banks have been blamed for increasing the general distrust by alarmist measures; but it is only fair to remember that the situation was so alarming because the Government had no plans ready for meeting it. If

[1] French Yellow Book (1914), p. 9.
[2] An authority has informed me that by July 31, 1914, only £4,250,000 had been acquired in gold.

Bank Holiday had not ensued, and been extended by three more days, an unparalleled panic might have been the result. Fortunately, the advice of financial experts led to the adoption of remedial measures such as the moratorium. The mere fact that so desperate a measure had to be adopted showed that the Government had prepared no plan for reassuring the Joint Stock Banks in case of a crisis. It is also noteworthy that the reserve of gold in the Bank of England had not been increased, as would certainly have been the case if a crisis had been expected. No scheme for paper notes was ready, and some little time elapsed before the issue of Treasury Notes which an amateur forger could not easily counterfeit. At Berlin everything had been thought out and provided. At London the City was caught in a state of trustful innocence.

Far worse, however, was the general political situation of the United Kingdom. The Germans seem to have been singularly impressed with the inability of our Government to deal with "the wild women." Much space was given in their papers to the outrages of the militants; and many were the comments on the softness and hesitancy of British procedure. The Germans, who never have any difficulty with their women, seem to have concluded that a Government which allowed itself to be hen-pecked, must be in its dotage. That was the general view in Germany; and it must be reckoned among the influences which produced a feeling of pride in the Fatherland and contempt for the decadent islanders.

The Irish Question produced an even deeper impression. That the British Government should be unable to prevent two sets of Irish Volunteers procuring arms and drilling was incomprehensible to the German mind. If it were possible I should like to have heard a lecture by Treitschke on that subject. Imagine the scorn he would pour forth on a State that could not control its citizens in the most elementary of political duties, and allowed them to pervert national defence into a national danger. A heavy responsibility lies somewhere about that whole business. That responsibility will be allotted someday and will prove to be an indirect cause of this war. One cannot but sympathize with the German private who was taken prisoner by an Irishman. At this he was most indignant. "What business have you fighting here (he said). You "ought to be fighting in your own civil war." I have received interesting proof that General Bernhardi himself had expected a civil war in Ireland. My informant allows me to quote the part of her letter bearing on this topic:—

LETCHWORTH.
Sept. 17, 1914.

It may possibly interest you to know that last April—May I spent at a Pension at Frascati, where I was next to General von Bernhardi and his wife at table. He asked me repeatedly about the Irish Question, showing great sympathy with the Nationalists; he also asked about the causes of the failure of the Government to deal successfully with the Suffragettes. All German men I met in Italy this winter seemed to take a special interest in these two points. . . .

This further point deserves notice. The Austrian Note to Serbia was sent on July 23, the day on which it became known that the Buckingham Palace Conference on the Irish Question was certain to fail.

It is now, I think, clear to anyone whose eyes are not blinded by preconceived notions, that the two Germanic

Empires chose the time with extreme skill for launching their bolt. Their method of clinching its effects will concern us in the next lecture. Here I wish to point out that the leaders of Germany, both in the spheres of thought and action, have always advocated an energetic initiative whenever a fit opportunity occurred. Treitschke represents the union of historical learning with the victorious militarism of 1870. He uses history as a text for glorifying Prussian procedure and stimulating its progress towards wider triumphs. He rejoices over the treatment of Saxony by Frederick the Great in 1756. "Should Frederick (he asks) have had respect for the "official regulations of Saxony?" Treaties? What are treaties? The State is superior to all treaties. Treitschke says: "The State cannot recognize an arbiter above "itself, and consequently legal obligations must in the "last resort be subject to its own judgment[1]." Which means that Prussia cannot be bound by international law if it thwarts her interests; also, that the rules of the Hague Conference are null and void so soon as the Prussian State feels the pinch of circumstances. That has been, not merely the dictum of a deaf professor; it is the maxim which has guided Prussia at most of the great crises since her first successful crime, the seizure of Silesia. Under good men like Frederick William III and IV and William I, she swerved nervously towards the Ten Commandments; but she afterwards recurred to the more gainful creed of Frederick the Great.

Let us look more closely at his procedure and that of Bismarck; for they are the chief exponents of Prussian State policy. Frederick made no attempt to justify his

[1] Treitschke, *Die Politik*, Bk I. § 3.

seizure of Silesia from the young Empress-Queen, Maria
Theresa, whom his father had lately sworn to uphold.
The young king struck quickly in 1740, and he left it to
his later apologists, including Carlyle, to discover justi-
fications. Frederick in his *Histoire de mon Temps* uses
no whitewash. He merely says that Maria Theresa was
weak; her army had of late been badly beaten by the
Turks; Russia for the time favoured him; and, as
France and England were always at feud, he would be sure
of the help of one of them. Therefore he struck at Silesia[1].

His action at the beginning of the Seven Years' War
is equally noteworthy. Here he had more reason for
striking. His enemies were preparing to move against
him, and he anticipated them. But he did so by over-
whelming an unoffending neutral that lay in his way,
Saxony. True, by that elaborate piece of mystification,
his *Mémoire raisonné*, he tried to show, later on, that
Saxony was conspiring against him: but the excuse
rings hollow, as hollow as those which William II sought
to foist on the world respecting Belgium. Frederick in
his *Histoire* supplies the real reason for the blow dealt
at Saxony: "Saxony not having finished her [military]
"arrangements, these conjunctures seemed favourable to
"gain advantages over the enemies, by forestalling them
"from the beginning of the campaign[2]." The British
Government, which did not want war in Europe, sought
to dissuade him from this precipitate action against
a neutral, but Frederick persisted. "Let us conquer" (he
said): "the politicians will then find plenty of justification
"for us." That phrase summed up his motives; and they
have largely governed Prussian policy ever since. It has

---

[1] Frédéric, *Hist. de mon Temps*, II. 54–6.　　　[2] *Ibid.* III. 37.

become a maxim at Berlin to make rapid use of the advantage which a central position gives to well-armed forces. In a strictly political sense the central position of Germany causes her anxiety. But every student of war knows that it confers great advantages if it be used with rapidity and decision. Therefore her policy at a crisis tends to be governed by military rather than diplomatic considerations. Prussian statesmen always remember those significant words in the will of Frederick the Great: "May this State always be governed with justice, wisdom and force[1]."

Much the same view was presented by the Prussian military writer, Clausewitz. For him the life of States was a constant struggle. When war broke out, it was only a change of method; the struggle for self-preservation then went on openly and by force. His notion of strategy is this: "The best strategy is always to be very strong, "firstly in general, and secondly, at the critical point." Thus, Prussia is always struggling. When she goes to war she merely intensifies and specializes her efforts with a view to the exhaustion of her enemy by the exercise of the utmost possible rigour. He thoroughly approved of Frederick's merciless use of Saxony in 1756–1762. All this was written in 1836–7, a time of profound peace[2].

The next great exponent of Prussian policy, Bismarck, modelled his policy on that of Frederick. It was strictly objective. He hated idealists. Of one of them he wrote thus in 1881: "Professor Gladstone perpetrates "one piece of stupidity after another. He has alienated

---

[1] Frédéric, *Hist. de mon Temps*, VI. 219.
[2] Clausewitz, *Vom Kriege und Kriegführung*, Bks I. Chs. 1, 2; VIII. Chs. 6, 7.

"the Turks: he commits follies in Afghanistan and at
"the Cape [the Majuba affair]; and he does not know how
"to manage Ireland. There is nothing to be done with
"him[1]." The part of Bismarck's career in which he
himself took most pride was the Schleswig-Holstein
Question, in which he got the better of many opponents,
brushed aside in succession all solutions but his own, and
had the satisfaction of seeing his handiwork completed
by an opportune attack upon Austria. His conduct of
Franco-Prussian negotiations in July 1870 was almost
equally skilful, for it led up to a rupture at a time ex-
ceedingly favourable to Prussia. Napoleon III was
known to be contemplating a league with Austria and
Italy with a view to an attack upon North Germany in
1871. Bismarck anticipated that attack; and, on the
plane of expediency, on which statesmen must act in such
a crisis, he was justified. Germany waged the war in a
straightforward way, and she deserved her triumph.

The wars of 1866–1870 are good examples of Prussian
policy. They were undertaken after a careful cal-
culation of chances and by a swift offensive. Whenever
Prussia wavered and acted weakly, as under Frederick
William II and III (at least in 1805–12), she came near
to ruin. The fate of Frederick William IV was even more
pitiable; for his plans were as diffuse as his decisions
were halting. Concentration of purpose on one practicable aim, and swiftness of action at the favourable
time, these have been the guiding principles of Prussia
at her most successful times. It is necessary to recall
these facts; for many persons who do not know them,
have formed curiously wrong judgments on Prussian

---

[1] *Bismarck; Some Secret Pages*, II. 456.

policy, and have framed for it apologies at which the men
of Berlin in their franker moods would be the first to
gibe. Treitschke and Bernhardi are excused as freaks,
alien to the German genius. True, they are to the
German genius in its best form, as typified by Goethe,
Kant, Schiller. But Imperial Germany is not now the
land of Goethe, Kant, Schiller. She is the creation of
William I and II, of Roon, Moltke, Bismarck and Krupp;
and she takes after her creators. A central State must,
of course, be cautious. Its policy cannot be swayed by
sentimental considerations. But since 1870 the German
frontier has been strong. It is extremely strong on the
side of France and equally so on that of Austria. Therefore in the new order of things there is less excuse for a
Machiavellian policy than there was in the days of
Frederick the Great. Fortified, too, by the Triple
Alliance with which Bismarck had buttressed her, she
might readily have relaxed her military rigour. But
the restless activity of William II has impelled her on
dangerous quests, which, as we have seen, involved acute
friction with Russia, Great Britain and Japan, while
alarming the United States and Portugal. At the same
time, too, he did nothing to relax the tension between
Germany and France. On the contrary, his rigorous
policy in Alsace-Lorraine made the friction worse.

    That was seen at the time of the Zabern outrage, when,
after trifling provocation, a neurotic young lieutenant drew
his sword on a lame shoemaker. The Chancellor and
Minister of War refused to censure him; and the protest
of the Reichstag, which at first passed a vote of censure,
was entirely ignored. The Military Court at Strassburg
quashed all legal proceedings; and it was seen that civil

law and a formal protest of the Reichstag counted as
nothing. The army ruled the State. That was clear in
the early days of 1914.

The excuse for all these proceedings was that Germany
must be armed to the teeth in order to confront Russia
and France; and that her policy may be explained as
prompted by fear. Let us examine this theory, not from
the utterances of private individuals (for they count as
nothing in Germany), but from the conduct of the Government, which alone is important in this connection.

There are two infallible tests by which you can tell a
fearful policy. It seeks to propitiate the most dangerous of its enemies; and it seeks to gain every possible
ally. Now, has Germany of late sought to propitiate
Russia? No sign can be found of any such intention,
since the Potsdam interview of November 1910. Then it
seemed for a time that Tsar and Kaiser had come to a
temporary accord. But, so soon as the Eastern Question
again became acute, Germany acted in direct opposition
to Russia's declared interests. She successfully opposed
Serbia and Montenegro in the Albanian dispute, and
finally she helped Austria in those insidious efforts which
wrecked the Balkan League, patched up an unsatisfactory
peace, and set the Turk on his feet once more. In all
this there was a direct defiance of Russia; and, what is
more, the two Germanic Empires succeeded. The years
1908, 1911 and 1913 are marked by three German successes,
Bosnia, the Morocco-Congo exchange, and the Treaty of
Bukharest[1]. Central Europe then gave the law to the

---

[1] Pan-Germans pronounced the acquisition of the large and fertile
district from the French Congo a defeat; but this only shows the extent
of their Moroccan designs.

Triple Entente, which bowed before the dictates of Berlin. In all this there is no sign of fear, rather of boundless confidence. This was seen by M. Jules Cambon, French ambassador at Berlin, who reported to his Government on May 6, 1913: "These people do not fear war: "they fully accept its possibility, and they have taken "their steps in consequence[1]."

Equally significant was the treatment of Italy by the Germanic Empires. It was notorious both in 1908 and in 1912–13 that Italy disliked their Balkan policy. Yet, save in the matter of the Sanjak of Novi-Bazar (1908), Italy had scant consideration at their hands. In truth, their policy seems to lay more stress on the friendship of the Sublime Porte than of the Cabinet of Rome. Certain it is that neither Berlin nor Vienna swerved from their designs in order to retain the alliance of Italy. That alliance was of a defensive nature, and was therefore forfeited if war resulted from their aggressive designs; yet they persisted in those designs, with the result that they must have foreseen, the loss of Italy's help. All this, I repeat, savours not of fear, but of blind confidence in their ability to carry out at all costs a preconceived policy, the hour for the execution of which had now sounded forth.

Finally, take the supreme test for Prussian policy, the disposition of her troops at the beginning of the war. Did that imply dread of Russia? On the contrary, Bernhardi, Frobenius and other officers have for some time past been declaring that Germany is perfectly well able to wage war on both fronts at once. They had built strategic railways, often four lines abreast, which

[1] French Yellow Book (1914), p. 12.

would enable large masses of men to be thrown quickly
on the eastern or the western frontier; and on the eastern
lines especially they have adopted a mechanical device
whereby their rolling-stock could quickly be adjusted to
the different gauge of some of the Russian lines. Of
course, they would not repeat Napoleon's blunder of
advancing far into Russia; but, if Austria offered vigorous
help, as she was certain to do after the murder of her
Archduke, the German Powers might hope to converge on
Warsaw and capture it before the unwieldy Eastern
Colossus had fully bestirred himself. The special circumstances of 1914, viz. the strike in Russia, afforded
special ground for hope that the Germans and Austrians
might not only capture Warsaw, but push on finally to
what is a good military position—the line of the Rivers
Niemen and Bug. There they might pause for the winter,
having weakened Russia by the occupation of Poland
and perhaps part of her Baltic provinces. But, far from
throwing their chief weight on the side of Russia, as they
would have done if they feared her, they sent their great
masses westwards to Belgium and France.

The supreme proof that they did not fear Russia is to
be found in this fact. Austria, which has more reason
than Germany to be apprehensive of Russia, sent a
considerable force, along with heavy siege guns into
Belgium and Northern France. True, the Central Powers
found out, when too late, that they had made a blunder
—that Belgium was not to be walked over in a week,
and Paris entered within three weeks. The resistance
in the west was more obstinate, the advance of the
Russians quicker, than the German Staff had expected.
But their miscalculation is a tribute to their excess of

confidence; and it suffices to explode the theory of fear
which has been so confidently set forth. The German
Staff summarized its programme thus: "We shall smash
"France in three weeks, then wheel about and deliver a
"knock-down blow to Russia before she has had time to
"complete her mobilization. Belgium will offer only the
"resistance of sullenness. England will not come in at
"all." That was the prospect held forth to encourage
the leaders of German industry; and it only slightly
exaggerates what we can now see to have been the plan
of campaign. That plan was based, not on fear, not even
on principles of ordinary prudence, but rather on the
feeling of supreme confidence expressed in the favourite
national song:

Deutschland, Deutschland, über alles, über alles in der Welt.

LECTURE VIII

THE RUPTURE

" Τότε δὲ καὶ νεότης πολλὴ μὲν οὖσα ἐν τῇ Πελοποννήσῳ, πολλὴ δ'
ἐν ταῖς 'Αθήναις, οὐκ ἀκουσίως ὑπὸ ἀπειρίας ἥπτετο τοῦ πολέμου."
(And then the young men being numerous in the Peloponnese, and
also at Athens, were, through inexperience, not unwilling to start
the war.)

THUCYDIDES, Bk II. ch. 8.

As we have seen, Austria despatched to Serbia a
series of exacting demands on the very day on which it
became known that the Buckingham Palace Conference
on Irish Affairs was certain to fail. So soon as that news
reached Berlin, the chances became in the highest degree
favourable to the Central Powers. The finances of France
showed a deficit of £32,000,000, and the Chambers had
reluctantly assented to the loan of £52,000,000, deemed
necessary for carrying through the Three Years' Service.
The Russian railways were likely to be paralysed by a
wide-spread strike; and the United Kingdom was on the
verge of a civil war. Thus, by July 23 a state of things
had come to pass far more favourable even than that
which Bernhardi had thus described:

When a State is confronted by the material impossibility of
supporting any longer the warlike preparations which the power
of its enemies has forced upon it; when it is clear that the rival

States must gradually acquire, from natural reasons, a lead that cannot be won back; when there are indications of an offensive alliance of stronger enemies who only await the favourable moment to strike—then the moral duty of the State towards its citizens is to begin the struggle while the prospects of success and the political circumstances are tolerably favourable[1].

Further, Germany could not wait much longer. The Junker party was resolved to get rid of the drastic succession duties recently outlined by the German Government. They were inevitable if the armed peace lasted; and the German governing class judged war to be preferable to such a peace. The Junkers were furious at the heavy financial burdens, with no territorial acquisitions to show for them. The French Minister at Munich in July, 1913, declared that public opinion would welcome war—"as the solution of political and economic difficulties "which will only become worse[2]."

Moreover, Austria was eager to attack the Serbs. Her Note of July 23 contained two demands which no independent State could accord; viz. to admit Austrian officials to take part in the trial of the Serbs accused of complicity in the murder at Serajevo; while other officials were to collaborate in the suppression of the anti-Austrian propaganda. The former of these demands Serbia rejected; the latter she promised to comply with so far as it agreed with the principles of international law, criminal procedure and neighbourly relations. To all the other demands she assented. To the two just named she could not assent without becoming a vassal State. In view of the exceptionally short interval of

[1] Bernhardi, *The Next War*, p. 52.
[2] French Yellow Book (1914), p. 13

48 hours allowed for a reply to far-reaching and complex
demands, Austria must have sought to provoke a war.
Such was the opinion of our ambassador at Vienna,
Sir Maurice de Bunsen, who stated that: "this country
"has gone wild with joy at the prospect of war with
"Serbia, and its postponement or prevention would
"undoubtedly be a great disappointment[1]." Whether
Austria would have welcomed a general war is a wider
question; but Russia had repeatedly warned the Court of
Vienna that any attack on Serbia must involve war with
Russia[2]. Therefore, that Government precipitated the
crisis with a full knowledge of the terrible consequences
that must ensue; and the question now arises—Would it
have acted thus if it had not received promises of powerful
support?

What was the influence of Germany in the developments of Hapsburg policy? Her Government has dis-
claimed all knowledge of the Austrian demands on Serbia.
But the following facts seem to imply adequate if not
exact knowledge on the part of some at least of her responsible Ministers. (1) A German official Note approving
Austria's demands was handed in at London by the
German Ambassador on July 24, a fact scarcely possible
unless the Cabinet of Berlin had previously known their
tenour. (2) The Italian Government, always on cool terms
with Austria, had cognizance of them on July 23. If so,
why had not the Government of Berlin, always closely
associated with that of Vienna? (3) On July 23, the
Bavarian Prime Minister stated that he knew the terms

---

[1] British White Paper, Nos. 5, 39, 41.
[2] *Ibid.*, No. 139; Russian Orange Book, Nos. 4, 5, 10, 13–16, 23.

of that Note[1]. (4) Von Tschirsky, German Ambassador
at Vienna, stated on July 26 that Germany "knew
"very well what she was about in backing up Austria-
"Hungary in this matter." (5) Sir Maurice de Bunsen
had good reason for believing that Tschirsky knew
the terms of the Austrian Note and telegraphed them
to Kaiser William[2]. These facts, taken together, con-
stitute a proof as complete as historical evidence generally
admits. There is also the curious fact, just revealed in
the French Official Correspondence (Yellow Book), that
von Jagow, German Secretary for Foreign Affairs, did
not think it worth while to read the Serbian reply to
Austria's demands, though on that reply depended peace
or war in the South-East[3]. Equally significant is it
that, on the Kaiser's hurried return from his Baltic cruise
to Berlin, Germany and Austria acted in unison. On the
28th Germany rejected the British proposal for a Conference, and on that day Austria declared war on Serbia.

As to the Powers forming the Triple Entente, they
were undoubtedly surprised by Austria's sudden action.
On July 23 the French President and the chief Ministers
of the Republic were at Cronstadt and entertained the
Tsar and his suite on board their warship *La France*.
President Poincaré and the Tsar both made friendly
speeches containing not a phrase that differed from the
ordinary. The Tsar referred to the Franco-Russian
alliance as a guarantee for peace which both nations
desired to perpetuate. At Paris a European war was far
from the thoughts of the public. The Caillaux Trial still
reigned supreme, witness the fact that the issue of the

[1] French Yellow Book (1914), p. 28.
[2] British White Paper, Nos. 9, 32, 38, 95.   [3] French Yellow Book, p. 69.

Figaro of July 24 allotted two columns to the Cronstadt fête, thirty-six columns to the Caillaux Trial, and two only to the Austrian Note to Serbia. The editorial comment ended with the declaration that the Great Powers would abstain from conflict; and it seemed that Russia was intimidated by Austria's energy.

Across the English Channel public attention was concentrated almost entirely on the preparations for civil war in Ireland. But on July 20 Sir Edward Grey asked the German ambassador, Prince Lichnowsky, what step Austria was about to take regarding Serbia, and advised Germany to urge moderation on the Court of Vienna. The prince gave a dubious reply. On July 22 von Jagow, Secretary of State for Foreign Affairs at Berlin, admitted to our ambassador, Sir Edward Goschen, that Austria was about to take action, and he claimed that it concerned no other Power whatever; and this, too, in spite of the repeated warnings of Russia to the Hapsburg Court that its attack on Serbia must involve war with Russia. In the face of these repeated warnings Germany held to her original contention, that the quarrel concerned Austria and Serbia alone. By this course of action the Berlin Government practically gave Austria *carte blanche.*

From this rigid attitude little hope of success could be augured for Sir Edward Grey's proposals (July 24–26) of a Conference, in which Great Britain and France, after deliberating with Germany and Italy, should endeavour to moderate the zeal of their respective Allies—Russia and Austria. Seeing that the war-fever at Vienna was arousing angry feelings at Petrograd, such a solution of the difficulty was perhaps the only one practicable.

France and Italy accepted it; while Russia expressed her approval. Germany declined, for reasons which must be pronounced frivolous, in view of the extreme gravity of the situation. The coincidence of her refusal with the aggravation of the crisis by a declaration of war against Serbia has already been noticed[1].

An alternative to Sir Edward Grey's proposal of a Conference was suggested concurrently at Petrograd on July 24, that is, three days before Austria declared war. It was as follows. Sazonoff, Russian Minister for Foreign Affairs, and the French ambassador at Petrograd, suggested that Great Britain ought at once to join France and Russia, the three Powers taking up "a firm and "united attitude," as the only means of averting war[2]. The question has by this time often been discussed whether that was the only means of averting war. That explanation is plausible. But such a course of action was open to grave objections. Firstly, our ambassador, Sir George Buchanan, to whom this difficult question was put, had no authorization to assent to it. The Triple Entente did not bind us to joint action—so much is clear; for otherwise the question would not have been put. But, apart from that, Great Britain could not consistently adopt a threatening tone towards the Central Powers when on

[1] British White Paper, Nos. 10, 11, 36, 42, 43, 49, 71.

[2] *Ibid.* No. 6; Russian Orange Book, No. 17. No. 23 shows that Russia sought to persuade Italy to mediate at Vienna in favour of peace. All documents yet published show Russia's desire for peace. No. 77 sets forth her case against Germany.

With the facts stated above, compare the assertion of the German Chancellor, on December 2, 1914, that our Government could have averted war "if it had without ambiguity declared at Petrograd that "Great Britain would not allow a continental war to develop from the "Austro-Serb conflict"!

that very day Sir Edward Grey had suggested a Conference
with a view to a friendly solution of the difficulty.   You
may either conciliate or threaten; you cannot do both at
once; and Sir Edward Grey, when the question was
referred to him from Petrograd, commended our ambassador's caution and continued to advocate the Conference.   He knew, far better than his critics can know,
that both Austria and Germany were in so irritable a
mood as to be likely to take extreme measures if anything
resembling a menace were used.   He therefore adhered to
the conciliatory proposal, which Germany was to reject
on the 28th.   By so doing she put herself in the wrong;
while unprejudiced observers noted that British policy was
not only pacific, but also calculated to allay the rising
storm of passion.

Most important of all considerations was the influence
which a menacing attitude would exert upon the Cabinet
of Rome.   There was to be found the key of the diplomatic
situation.   Relatively to the Central Powers, Italy held a
position not unlike that of Great Britain with regard to
the Triple Entente.   True, she was more closely attached,
but her obligations were of a defensive nature.   If,
however, we joined Russia and France and issued a
threatening declaration to the Central Powers, the immediate result must have been to tighten the bonds of
the Triple Alliance.   Therefore conciliation was not merely
the only consistent and morally justifiable course; it was
also the prudent course.   In truth those who now say
that a sterner attitude should have been taken towards
the Germanic Powers advocate what was, in the circumstances, a weaker course of action.   They confuse
diplomacy with war, where the offensive is generally the

stronger alternative, whereas in diplomacy it is generally
the weaker alternative. It was so in this case. Italy,
noting that her Allies persistently adopted an aggressive
tone, was perfectly justified in parting company with
them. On August 3 the Italian Government stated that,
the action of the Central Powers having been aggressive,
the Triple Alliance lapsed, and Italy would remain
neutral[1]. That decision, I repeat, could not have been
formed if we had joined France and Russia in a declaration
to the Central Powers which could have been represented
as a menace. The nation therefore owes a deep debt of
gratitude to Sir George Buchanan and Sir Edward Grey
for their self-restraint in declining a course of action
which on the surface seemed attractive. If they had
followed it, war would not have been averted, and we
should now be fighting Italy. A study of this question
must yield cause for thankfulness that our foreign policy
has not been directed by brilliant and self-confident
amateurs, who claim to possess an exceptional fund of
common sense.

Meanwhile, as we have seen, Kaiser William had
returned in haste from his Baltic cruise, greatly to the
regret of the German Foreign Office, which affected
solicitude for the excitement likely to be produced by
that step[2]. The fact of its regret may be noted, the
excuse may be disregarded. Late on July 28 (the day of
Austria's declaration of war) Kaiser William telegraphed
to the Tsar. After referring to the murders of King

[1] British White Paper, Nos. 49, 64, 92, 152.
[2] The arguments urged in Germany as to the Kaiser knowing nothing
of diplomatic developments during his cruise are clearly inapplicable to
the age of wireless telegraphy

Alexander and his Queen in 1903, and to that of the
Archduke Francis Ferdinand, he continued: "Un-
"doubtedly you will agree with me, that we two, you and
"I as well as all sovereigns, have a common interest in
"insisting that all those morally responsible for this
"terrible murder shall suffer deserved punishment."
He therefore expressed the hope that the Tsar would not
be overborne by the excitement on behalf of Serbia which
was increasing in Russia. The Tsar replied on the
following day: "...In this serious moment I ask you
"urgently to help me. A disgraceful war has been de-
"clared on a weak nation. The indignation at this,
"which I fully share, is immense in Russia. I foresee
"that soon I can no longer withstand the pressure that is
"being brought to bear upon me, and that I shall be
"forced to adopt measures which will lead to war. In
"order to prevent such a calamity as a European War, I
"ask you in the name of our old friendship, to do all
"that is possible for you to prevent your ally from going
"too far." The Kaiser returned to the charge with two
telegrams. In the former he repeated his former argument
and added: "it is quite possible for Russia to remain in
"her rôle of a spectator towards the Austro-Serbian War,
"without dragging Europe into the most terrible war
"that it has ever seen[1]." The ground on which the
Kaiser based this charge was that on July 29 Russia had
mobilized part of her army (viz. in the military districts
of Odessa, Kieff, Moscow, and Kazan) as a sharp warning
to Austria. The Kaiser deprecated this mobilization

[1] German White Book, Annexes 20–23 A. For Serbia's appeal to
Russia for help see Russian Orange Book, No. 6. No. 56 shows that
the Tsar *on July* 28 telegraphed a reply in the affirmative.

(albeit only partial) obviously because it would interfere
with the pre-arranged plan of an Austrian incursion into
Serbia, with which no outsider had any concern.   To this
scheme he adhered with the rigidity which forms a prominent feature of his character.   As his study of Napoleon
has finally endowed him with a full measure of Napoleonic
pertinacity, we may pause to notice its manifestation in
a physical sense.   On the occasion of a religious service
before the troops on parade, it was noticed that, while
everyone else occasionally shifted the weight of the body
from one leg to the other, the Kaiser remained absolutely
inflexible during the whole of the hour.   It was his manner
of doing honour to the Hohenzollern Deity.   Now, the
will-power which so prolonged a strain implies has been
exerted increasingly on foreign policy, all the more so
because the present Chancellor is inexperienced in diplomatic affairs[1].

In its psychological aspect, then, the crisis may be
stated thus: the fate of Europe depended on the ability
of the Kaiser to realize the extreme peril of the course
which he was following, that is, if he was, as he claimed,
the friend of peace.   If so, he completely misjudged the
situation, mainly (it would seem) because he staked all
on being able to convince the Tsar that all sovereigns
had a common interest in assuring the chastisement of a
nation of assassins.   But here again he displayed another
defect, excess of energy.   He urged this plea with so much
insistence that the Tsar must have discerned in it an
appeal to his fears.   Certainly, he rejected it most
decisively, and he took his stand on what may be termed
the national ground.   As the father of his people he

[1] Lamprecht, pp. 82, 110.

could not see a small Slav State dragooned by Austria.
Knowing the history of her efforts, from 1878 onwards,
to secure hold of Serbia, he saw in the present appeals
merely a repetition in acuter form, of the Germanic
policy which had inflicted defeats on the Slav cause in
1908 and 1912–13. Twice he had bowed before the
Kaiser's "shining armour." He was resolved not to
endure humiliation a third time and see Austria overrun
the Balkans. That she was aiming at the longed-for
goal, Salonica, was reported both at Rome and Constantinople. At the latter place the Austrian ambassador
bemoaned "the deplorable situation of Salonica under
"Greek administration," and then spoke of the "assistance
"on which an Austrian army could count from Mussulman
"population discontented with Serbian rule[1]." While
the Tsar was being amused by professional disquisitions
on the duties of crowned heads, the Austrian eagle was
about to wing its flight to Salonica.

If there was any danger of the Tsar succumbing to
the appeals from Potsdam, it vanished on receipt of the
news as to secret and swift preparations for war in
Germany, which were proceeding on both fronts. This
was the more threatening, as the French President and
Ministers did not reach France, after their voyage from
Cronstadt, until July 27–28, up to which time no Minister
was able to give definite orders. The absence of the
Government and the general confusion in the administration, presented an opportunity such as had never occurred since the year 1875. Then, as we saw in Lecture I,
Russia and Great Britain declared that France must
not be taken at a disadvantage; and, now again, as the

[1] British White Paper, Nos. 19, 82.

situation developed, Russia saw the danger to her ally. On July 31 she ordered a general mobilization. This led to instant ultimatums from Berlin to Petrograd and Paris, requesting demobilization under pain of the commencement of hostilities.

The circumstances amidst which these imperious demands were sent deserve notice. On July 31 Russia signified both to the Austrian and British Governments her desire to frame an amicable arrangement with the Court of Vienna, in accordance with the plan suggested by Sir Edward Grey. That Court forthwith assented; and consequently there appeared a prospect of a peaceable settlement. The attitude of Russia had throughout been conciliatory, and Austria now seemed about to respond in the same spirit. Then it was that Germany intervened, allowing Russia only twelve hours in which to agree to a complete demobilization. In the words of Jules Cambon, French ambassador at Berlin,—"The "ultimatum of Germany, intervening just at the exact "time at which agreement appeared on the point of "being established between Vienna and Petrograd, is "significant of her bellicose policy." Further, the incident, distinctly aggressive on her part, could be represented by her as implying general disarmament (though her own preparations were far advanced)—a plea which would for the time cajole her Social Democrats[1]. Germany, however, claims that Russia was arming fast before July 31, and without the Tsar's knowledge. On this question it is impossible at present· to acquire exact information.

[1] French Yellow Book, pp. 5, 13 15–17, 41, 66–9, 109. 110; Russian Orange Book, pp. 48–57.

Russia refused to accede to the German demand: France temporized, in the hope of gaining a day or two of respite. But the rupture came about on August 3; with Russia on August 1[1].

The storm-centre now moved suddenly to Belgium. Already, on July 29, the German Chancellor had made to Sir Edward Goschen his "infamous proposals," to the effect that, in the event of war, and provided that Great Britain maintained neutrality, Germany would take no mainland territory from France but limit her demands to French colonies. He further promised to respect the neutrality of Holland. As regards Belgium he said: "It "depended upon the action of France what operations "Germany might be forced to enter upon in Belgium, but, "when the war was over, Belgian integrity would be "respected if she had not sided against Germany[2]." The last clause is to be noted, because by the custom of nations, Belgium is bound to uphold her neutrality if it is impugned.

This stipulation is, indeed, an essential condition of neutrality; for otherwise a neutral State becomes a means whereby one State may attack another at a comparatively unguarded part of its frontier. The neglect to maintain neutrality had been the ruin of Poland. Moreover, at the end of August, 1870, when threatened by the powerful armies of Germany and France, Belgium had maintained her neutrality; and Marshal McMahon's forces, because they respected that neutrality, became wedged into a false position at Sedan. Further, in 1842 and 1875 (as

[1] British White Paper, Nos. 99, 105, 134. See M. P. Price, *Diplomatic History of the War* (1914), pp. 90—114 for military moves, etc.

[2] British White Paper, No. 85.

we have seen), statesmen, who discussed the question of
Belgium's neutrality, agreed that she would fulfil the
duties which it imposed. Early in 1852, Queen Victoria
wrote to the King of the Belgians, assuring him against
the alleged designs of Napoleon III, and stating—" Any
" attempt on Belgium would be *casus belli* for us[1]." In
1875 Bismarck admitted that Great Britain, as one of
the signatory Powers of the treaty of 1839 (constituting
Belgium a neutral State under international guarantees)
must defend Belgium if she were attacked. That was
consonant with the declaration of Mr Gladstone in 1870,
though he phrased it with less clearness than could be
desired.

It is also well known that the German Staff discussed
questions arising from the possible forcing of the Scheldt
estuary (in Dutch waters) by a British expedition, which
might seek to succour the Belgian army if driven into its
great camp of refuge at Antwerp. Those discussions pre-
supposed that Great Britain would make the attempt.
Further, the Dutch Government had mounted heavy guns
at Flushing to command that estuary, as if it feared some
such action by the British. Its action was deemed unfriendly both to Great Britain and to Belgium, especially
as it neglected to fortify the Dutch-German frontier.

Consequently the military and naval situation, no less
than the diplomatic engagements, proclaimed the fact
that Great Britain was bound in honour to protect
Belgium if she were attacked, and that both at Berlin and
The Hague it was expected that she would in that case
defend her by force of arms. The Belgian Government
also, on July 24, expressed the confident belief that Great

---

[1] *Letters of Queen Victoria*, II. p. 438.

Britain and the other signatory Powers would act in that manner. For its part, it intended to uphold the neutrality of Belgium, "whatever the consequences." Preparatory measures of defence were also adopted to give effect to this appeal for the support of the Powers. Belgium had every right to expect that her appeal would be respected because, of the four States which have been permanently neutralized by international law, viz. Switzerland (1815), Belgium (1831, 1839), Luxemburg (1867), the [Belgian] Congo (1885), not one has been attacked. On the contrary, in the case of Belgium, on every occasion on which she appealed to the treaty constituting her a neutral State, that treaty was respected, even in less important matters[1]. History will therefore record the verdict that, during 99 years, there has occurred no violation of the territory of an internationally neutralized State, and that Germany has been the first nation since Waterloo to commit such a violation. To find a parallel, we must go back to the ages of barbarism.

As regards the conduct of Great Britain at the crisis, Germans, from the Kaiser downwards, have affected so much surprise that a few words seem called for as to our action in times past when the independence of the Low Countries was threatened by a Great Power.

I must almost apologize for the hackneyed nature of the facts I am about to name. Since the reign of Edward I

---

[1] E. Descamps, *La Neutralité de la Belgique* (1902), pp. 335, 552. Professor Westlake (*Review of International Law*, 1901), states that neither the neutral State nor any of the signatories can annul the obligations which the original compact imposes. See, too, Descamps, *L'État neutre à Titre permanent* (Paris and Brussels, 1912), ch. v, § 6. On April 29, 1914, von Jagow assured the Reichstag Committee that Belgian neutrality would be respected.

no English ruler, endowed with energy and patriotism, has allowed a Great Power to conquer or annex the Flemish and Dutch provinces. Our first important naval battle, that off Sluys (1337), was fought to keep the French out of Flanders. The names of Sir Philip Sidney, Cromwell, Marlborough, and Wellington, further recall to us the numerous campaigns whereby Britons assured either the independence of those provinces, or at least, their governance by Austria on terms not unfavourable to them and productive of security to England. On the other hand, hostile Powers have from early times sought to possess those coasts whence an invasion of our shores can most readily be attempted.

To resume: the following facts are clear and indisputable: (1) Belgian neutrality had never yet been violated; (2) apart from sinister plans in 1866 and 1875, the signatories to the fundamental pact of 1839 had always been prepared to fulfil their obligations to Belgium; (3) the defence of the Low Countries against aggression by any Great Power is the most prominent and persistent feature of British foreign policy from the time of Edward I to that of George V. The events leading to the many battles fought in the Netherlands, from Sluys to Waterloo, were manifestations of the same motive, which led us to protest against the construction of Dutch forts dominating the Scheldt estuary, while Holland did not defend her eastern frontier against Germany. This guiding principle of British policy is, I repeat, so obvious, so well known to every historical student, that it cannot be unknown to statesmen and publicists in Germany. Accordingly, we are justified in branding as hypocritical the clamour which has there been raised against us for taking a step which honour and

sound policy alike prescribed[1]. That German professors
should take the lead in these outbursts of malice is not
the least extraordinary incident amidst all the mad events
of this *annus mirabilis*. Further, that the German
Chancellor, Bethmann-Hollweg, should ever have made to
a British ambassador the cynical proposals of July 29 is
to be explained by his total inexperience in diplomatic
affairs, for which Professor Lamprecht vouches[2].

As to the stories of the violation of Belgian neutrality
by British or French troops, or aviators, whereby German
officials and journalists sought to excuse Germany's proceedings towards Belgium, they are sufficiently refuted,
firstly, by the bewildering inconsistencies of the stories
themselves[3], and secondly, by the action of the Chancellor,
who, when those inconsistencies were patent even at Berlin,
took refuge in the statement that necessity knows no law,
and that it was absolutely essential for Germany to "hack
"her way through," *i.e.* to Paris. Here at least there
was no pretence. Bethmann-Hollweg may at least claim
the merit of having stated the usual Prussian procedure
with the usual Prussian frankness. But the measure of
his political intelligence may be grasped by the incoherent
fury which he displayed towards Sir Edward Goschen at
their final interview. A statesman who had the faintest

[1] The Chancellor's speech to the Reichstag on December 2 is a tissue
of falsehoods as will be seen by the British, French, and Russian State
Papers. How can he maintain that the British, unprovoked, suddenly
attacked unsuspecting Germany, when, on July 26, she suddenly re-
called her fleet from Norway, a step which led to our countermanding,
on July 27, the demobilization of the British fleet? The *Königin
Luise* began mine-laying off Felixstowe within fourteen hours of the
declaration of war.

[2] Lamprecht, p. 110.

[3] *e.g.* Belgian Grey Book, Nos. 21, 22.

consciousness of the blunders which had brought Great Britain into the field, would have sought to retrieve those blunders and render an accommodation possible at an early date.

Perhaps the explanation of this inconceivable folly may be found in the priority accorded to military considerations at that time. It is probable that, during the Kaiser's cruise, those considerations triumphed over the dictates of complaisance towards an ally (Italy) and neutrals, which diplomacy enjoins. The international situation was sufficiently complex to call for prudence and self-restraint. But a decision in favour of rapid and aggressive action at all costs was evidently formed by the close of July. The Kaiser on his return threw in his lot with the forward party and used his influence to cajole Russia while his western army dealt a smashing blow at Paris. The Meuse Valley via Namur had long been approved by soldiers as the quickest and easiest line of advance to the French capital. The 16-inch howitzers which Krupp had kept secret were with reason expected to demolish all fortifications except the very few of the most modern type. If, therefore, Belgium resisted, she would easily be trampled down; and the estimate of three weeks for the victory over France was not extravagant in view of the complete equipment and vast numbers of the German forces of the west. Everything had been provided—maps of Belgium for the soldiery, concrete foundations outside the Belgian fortresses, while Krupp had withheld from Antwerp some of the heavy guns long before ordered for the completion of its defences. On the River Scheldt above Antwerp had been erected a large and solidly built German factory, which proved at

the crisis to be furnished with abundance of heavy timber
and other appliances that enabled the invaders rapidly to
cross the river and thus harass the retreating Belgian and
British forces[1].   Other proofs might be cited as to the
careful preparations for invading the whole of Belgium,
not merely the Meuse Valley as was at first supposed.
The project was, not merely to strike at Paris, but to
acquire Antwerp, Ostend, and the northern ports of
France.

This fact, which is now obvious enough, is referred to
here because it throws light on the procedure of Bethmann-
Hollweg on July 29 in the interview already described.
He then offered to Sir Edward Goschen that Belgium
should recover her independence if she had not opposed
the Germans during their march.   That a brave people
should not at some points oppose the invaders, if the
due amount of rigour be adopted, is inconceivable; but,
even supposing that the Belgians had not resisted, their
doom was sealed; for the custom of nations does not
recognize a neutrality which its possessor does not uphold.
Therefore the German Chancellor's proposals could have
but one end in view, annexation.

His proposals were assessed by the British Government
at their due value, and on July 30 were decisively rejected.
So, too, was his proposal of a general neutrality agreement
between the two Powers; and the revelations made by
Mr Asquith on October 2 as to the manner in which
Germany had previously used that expedient so as to tie
our hands in face of all eventualities, sufficiently explain
the motive underlying the not dissimilar proposal of

[1] *Figaro*, Nov. 7, 1914.

July 29. It was evidently a bait wherewith to hook us while Germany worked her will on Belgium[1].

Sir Edward Grey now requested both the French and German Governments to give assurances of their respect for Belgian neutrality. The reply of France was so frank and complete as to refute the stories of French aggression. That of Germany to both the Belgian and British ambassadors was unsatisfactory. On July 31 von Jagow, the Foreign Secretary, declared to the former that Germany had no intention whatever of violating Belgian territory, but he could not make a declaration to that effect without prejudicing the chances of Germany in the event of war ensuing[2]. (It was the day of her ultimatum to France.) To Sir Edward Goschen he replied thus: He thought that any reply the German Ministers might give "could not but disclose a certain amount of "their plan of campaign, in the event of war ensuing, "and he was therefore very doubtful whether they would "return any answer at all." His surmise was correct. True, on August 1, Prince Lichnowsky made to Sir Edward Grey certain offers, to which some importance has been attached in certain quarters, but, as they contradicted the declarations of his chiefs at Berlin, they must be dismissed as possessing no official character. The divergence between his statements and that of his Government had previously been noticeable. On August 1 it was most marked[3].

During that interview with Prince Lichnowsky, Sir Edward Grey stated that the British Government

---

[1] British White Paper, Nos. 85, 101.
[2] Belgian Grey Book, Nos. 9, 11–13.
[3] British White Paper, Nos. 43, 46, 122, 123.

was not committed to any course of action, an assertion
consonant with his previous declarations, that the Austro-
Serb dispute in no way concerned us[1]. It is also worthy
of notice that, on August 2, Sir Edward Grey, in giving to
the French envoy, M. Cambon, the promise of our naval
support in case the French fleet were attacked by that
of Germany, was careful to add that that offer was subject
to the assent of the British Parliament. The fact proves
that the Entente with France, which is believed to refer
almost entirely to naval affairs, does not and cannot
override the authority of Parliament[2].

Matters now came swiftly to the climax. On August 2
Germany sent her troops into Luxemburg; but, as she
represented that act as prompted solely by administrative
reasons so as to prevent the French making use of the
railway through the Grand Duchy, Great Britain did
not treat that infraction of neutrality as constituting a
casus belli. Further, it did not vitally affect the safety
of France, as was the case when Germany proceeded to
violate Belgian neutrality[3]. On August 3 she demanded
permission from Belgium to despatch troops into that
land. Her pretext now was that this proceeding would
help Belgium to prevent the violation of her territory.
But, as by this time France had given an explicit promise
to respect Belgian neutrality (a fact which was already
perfectly well known at Berlin[4]), the Government of
Brussels at once detected the hollowness of the pretext;

---

[1] British White Paper, Nos. 87, 116, 119.

[2] *Ibid.* No. 148.

[3] As Prussia in 1867 withdrew her troops from Luxemburg (where
she had them since 1815) she had some slight claim to reoccupy it in
time of crisis. (See Descamps, p. 73.)

[4] British White Paper, No. 122.

and it is in the light of this monstrous demand on Belgium
that we must view the eager appeal of the German Chancellor to Great Britain on August 4th, to remain neutral,
while German troops overran Belgium[1]. His despatch
was preceded by one from King Albert containing a manly
appeal for the support which Great Britain had always
accorded, especially in 1870 during the Franco-Prussian
War. British support was, of course, forthcoming; but
Sir Edward Grey made one more effort to convince the
German Government of the seriousness of the step which
it was then contemplating. On hearing that German
troops had entered Belgium, he despatched an ultimatum,
demanding that Germany should respect the neutrality
of Belgium, on pain of encountering the hostility of the
United Kingdom. As the Court at Berlin refused to draw
back, war ensued at the end of August 4.

It has been suggested that he should have declared
more emphatically at an earlier stage what our conduct
would be in such a crisis. To this it will suffice to reply
that any declaration on his part which assumed that
Germany was about to violate Belgian soil, while she was
hotly disclaiming any such intention, would have aggravated the crisis, instead of averting it. He made it as
clear as diplomatic procedure admits, that Great Britain
regarded the Belgian Question as one of extreme gravity,
on which we must, at the worst, take decisive action.
Moreover, the fact that the British fleet was kept together, instead of dispersing for the manœuvres, was
a circumstance calculated to make more impression on
the statesmen at Berlin than any number of diplomatic
representations. They therefore have no ground for

[1] British White Paper, No. 157.

complaining that they were not duly warned. On the
whole, British diplomacy may be pronounced to have
steered steadily a middle course such as ought to have
averted a collision. If it failed, it was because the men
at Berlin were resolved at all costs to carry out their plans
as regards Belgium. Again, the final verdict on British
versus German diplomacy came from Rome. The Italian
statesmen were far better judges of the merits of the
dispute than any outsiders can be; and their action
tells decisively in favour of the conduct of the United
Kingdom[1].

In view of the facts set forth in this and former lectures,
and still more in those of the French, Belgian, and Russian
despatches, which I have been unable to compress into
these lectures, no reasonable person can entertain any
doubt as to the aggressive designs of Germany. She
intended first to crush France, then to repel the Russian
forces and wage defensive campaigns in East Poland
which would wear out Russia. The Kaiser's telegrams to
the Tsar may have been designed to postpone the Russian
mobilization, which he expected in any case to be slow
owing to the strike. That he desired to avert war with
Russia is inconceivable in view of his action in sending
the imperious ultimatum of July 31. Russia was bound
by honour to succour France, who was known to be in
deadly danger[2]. She was equally bound to try to save
Serbia from the Austrian forces then at her gates. Therefore the Kaiser must have counted either on disgracing
Russia in the eyes of the world, or on compelling her to

[1] See speech of Italian Premier in *Times* of Dec. 5, 1914.
[2] British White Paper, Nos 99, 105; French Yellow Book, Nos. 106,
114, 118, 127.

fight at a time equally favourable to himself and unfavourable to the Tsar.

His conduct towards Great Britain was somewhat of the same nature. If his Chancellor's proposals of July 29 had been accepted, Great Britain would forthwith have felt the paralysing sense of shame which is more deadly than fifty defeats. Disgraced in the eyes of the world, stricken in all probability with civil war, she would easily have succumbed in the final round of the world-conflict. For it is inconceivable, having regard to the Kaiser's lengthy and laborious intrigues in Turkey[1] and South Africa that he was not seeking for an opportunity to overthrow his chief antagonist. The British Empire met him everywhere; and his restless spirit, like that of his far greater exemplar, could not brook a state of things in which the British race occupied the best lands of the world. From the standpoint of a German Chauvinist the conflict between the two Empires was inevitable; but the eager precipitation of Germany in clutching at Antwerp and Ostend, disclosed her ulterior designs and brought into the field the Island Power which, up to the end of July, steadily refused to believe in the imminence of war.

If all Germans are Chauvinists then the war was unavoidable; and it is now known from the Secret Report of the German Government that in the spring and summer of 1914 official influence was used in order to excite public opinion to the state of exaltation in which war was acclaimed as ushering in the hour of Germany's greatness. If, I say, this is the permanent conviction of the German

[1] Note the naïve admission of the German Chancellor in his speech of December 2, that the Turks were obliged to join in the war.

people, then war will possibly be the occupation of the
human race during as long a period as occurred under the
baneful sway of Napoleon I.

But surely defeat must bring calmer thoughts. The
Germans must cease to plan a *Weltpolitik* that endangers
the existence of Great Britain, France, Belgium, Holland,
Russia, the Balkan States, and Japan, probably, also, of
the United States.   In Talleyrand's famous phrase they
must cease to be world-conquerors and become "good
"Europeans."   They will, before long, realize that the
régime of force, which three triumphant wars have taught
them to acclaim as the chief factor in German progress,
must lead to disaster.   In the nature of things, force
begets force; and the vaster and more aggressive the
schemes championed by their War-Lord, the more certain
is it that other nations will unite to resist them to the very
death.   That is the outstanding lesson of the events of a
century ago in which Prussia bore her part nobly against
schemes of universal domination.   The songs of Arndt and
the exploits of Blücher, to which she now appeals on behalf
of her war of conquest, ought to recall her to the ideals
of national independence and of resistance to an aggressive
imperialism, for which a century ago she strove shoulder
to shoulder with the British and Russian soldiery.   Of
late she has been maddened by the lust of conquest which
brought ruin to Napoleonic France.   Let her hark back
from Treitschke to Niebuhr, from Nietzsche to Fichte,
from

"Deutschland, Deutschland, über alles, über alles in der Welt,"
to *Die Wacht am Rhein*.

In that happier day, which is surely ahead after these
horrors are past, Germany will, it is to be hoped, discover

that international law, on which she has insanely trampled, may prove to be her safest support. For when the din of war dies down, we shall realize that behind the lust of conquest there was an elemental force impelling the German people forward. Their population is ever increasing; and they must have more elbow-room in some of the sparsely inhabited lands. On this occasion they have sought the disastrously wrong method of war. Just as Napoleon the Great mercilessly exploited the nascent strength of French democracy, so, too, his imitator has now made use of the natural desire of his people for expansion to bring about conflicts of even wider extent and greater fury. In both cases the methods employed were disastrous; but we must recognize the naturalness of the impelling force behind both Emperors. A century ago there was no Supreme Court of Appeal as to the vital interests of nations. To-day there is such a Court, the Hague Tribunal. The wiser and better course for Germany would have been to seek to enlarge its powers so as to include the consideration of her important vital problem, and the adoption of some scheme which promised a peaceful solution.

In the course of the reaction in favour of international law, to which its insane violation must lead, the Hague Tribunal will surely acquire an added dignity, a wider scope, and surer guarantees, in the discharge of its beneficent functions. The task will, doubtless, prove to be difficult; and cynics will point to the Holy Alliance of the monarchs as a warning example. But, though three or four monarchs failed ninety years ago, may not the collective wisdom of all the nations now succeed? For my part I cannot believe that the ingenuity of the

human race, which has lately gone so largely towards
perfecting the means of slaughter, must always fail in
providing a remedy for slaughter.   The enlarged and
strengthened Areopagus of the nations must and will
discuss such questions as the excessive pressure of population in one State, and it will seek to direct the surplus
to waste or ill-cultivated lands.   In that more intelligent
and peaceful future Germans will not need to "hack their
way through."   The fiat of mankind will, I hope, go
forth that they shall acquire, if need be, parts of Asia
Minor, Mesopotamia, and South Brazil.   America will
realize that the world cannot for ever bow down to the
Monroe Doctrine, especially as the United States have
become a colonising Power, but that parts of South
America may safely be thrown open to systematic coloni-
sation by a nation like Germany.   Above all, the Council
of the Nations will decide that an effete rule like that of
the Turks must give way before that of more progressive
peoples.   If this is the outcome of the present awful
conflict, it will not have been waged wholly in vain.

NOTE. On December 5, 1914 the Italian Premier, Signor
Giolitti, declared that Austria, on August 9, 1913, announced
privately to Germany and Italy her intention of proceeding against
Serbia. Italy refused to co-operate. It is clear, then, that Austria's
coup of July 23, 1914 had long been planned, and that the murder
of the Archduke afforded the pretext.

APPENDIX I. SHIPBUILDING PROGRAMMES OF ENGLAND, GERMANY, AND FRANCE

(compiled by permission of Mr Frederick Jane, from his *Fighting Ships of the World*)

Year	1903–4			1904–5			1905–6			1906–7			1907–8			1908–9			1909–10			1910–11			1911–12		
Country	E.	G.	F.	E.	G.	F.	E.	G.	F.	E.	G.	F.	E.	G.	F.	E.	G.	F.	E.	G.	F.	E.	G.	F.	E.	G.	F.
Dreadnoughts and Super-Dreadnoughts				2	0	0	4	2	0	3	2	0	3	3	0	2	4	0	8	4	2	7	4	2	5	4	3
Pre-Dreadnoughts	5	1	4	0	4	0				0	0	2	0	0	4												
Armoured Cruisers	4	1	1	3	1	0	0	1	1	0	1	1															
Protected Cruisers and Scouts							0	3	0	0	2	0	1	2	0	6	2	0	6	2	0	5	2	0	5	2	0
Destroyers							6	6	6	2	12	8	5	12	5	16	12	7	24	12	7	20	12	8	20	12	0
Torpedo Boats							12	0	0	12	0	0	12	0	0							0	0	2			
Submarines							10	0	10	8	1	2	12	3	0	5	4	5	5	4	0	?	?	?	?	?	?

APPENDIX II

GERMAN PLANS IN SOUTH-WEST AFRICA

(Extracts reprinted by permission from the London Weekly Journal,
" South Africa.")

(By the Special Commissioner of the *Transvaal Chronicle*, in the autumn
of 1912.)

No. 6.

It is common knowledge amongst all Germans on the spot
that Bismarck's aim and desire was to effect a footing in South
Africa—*i.e.* the Transvaal, even if at the risk of insult to the
Boer Government in the days long gone by. Baulked, however,
by the fact of the Bechuanaland annexation, the scheme to
construct a strategical railway from the Swakop *viâ* Windhoek
to Johannesburg failed. So did a further scheme by which
"a few regiments of Prussian soliders could be landed at
Delagoa Bay to force a passage into the Transvaal!" (*vide* a
Transvaal Secret Service document). The amount of ammunition near Angra Pequena in 1883 gave rise to grave suspicion
at the Foreign Office in Downing Street, for the country had
once been British, and movements of troops, etc., in 1885 were
watched by British officers after the quitting of Palgrave at
the outbreak of the Hottentot and Herero wars in 1887.

No. 7.

There are ten thousand trained German soldiers in German
South-West Africa. Arms, ammunition, military supplies,
and stores to last an army of 10,000 men, fully equipped, for
six years, are now being rushed into the country. Five
thousand trained soldiers, with military equipment and stores
for two years, are now concentrated within 150 miles of the
Union border. German official statistics show that there are

only 8000 native males above the age of 15 in the whole
southern portion of the country, and nearly all north of the
area where the troops are concentrated. These natives possess
no rifles, and two-thirds are in military camps under constant
police supervision. There are about 30,000 adult native
males in the northern portion of the country. The Germans
assert that they are afraid of outbreaks among these natives
of the north. It would take two days at the most to bring a
strong German force to the Union frontier. It would take 14
days to bring a similar force from where they are concentrated
to this "dangerous" area. The force concentrated near the
Union border is therefore not intended for such native disturbances. What is it there for?

Recently several inspired German papers have demanded
an increase in the South-West African naval squadron and
garrison. At present the number of men serving with the
regular forces in German South-West Africa is 2300. But we
must not forget that nearly 2000 German men enter the country
annually, of whom a large number are officials. Every one of
these is a trained soldier. Recently there has been a particu-
larly keen official search through the country for all German
subjects fit for instant military service. In fact, unusual
activity prevails. Many young fellows are trying to get out
of liability for service by escaping to the Cape.....

The white population of German South-West Africa in
January, 1910, according to official statistics, was 11,791; of
these 8960 are males, an increase of males of 2996 as compared
with the year previous. There has been an equally great
increase since. The numbers given include the military.
About 10,000 men can now take the field, and provision is
made for 10,000 in guns, ammunition, supplies, and provisions
now being stored in the country.

A glance at the bills of lading for 1910 shows that to every
white man, woman, and child provisions equal to five and
three-quarter tons are imported into the country. These
bills of lading are guarded almost sacredly, and access to them
is only possible by scheming and bribing the officials in charge
of them. Why? Because the military supplies are not
published under the heading of imports, but only what is
being imported by the civil population. This is significant,
and must be borne in mind when speaking of military supplies.

At the present moment a six years' supply of provisions and other stores is stored at a point north of Aus, 180 miles from the coast, 400 miles travelling from Raman's Drift, on the Union frontier. The idea is that should a foe land at Lüderitz Bay the population could be brought up within a day, some 120 miles of railway blown up, the condensers destroyed, thus leaving the enemy a long time without water in the desert sands around Angra Pequena.....

Now, German officers and civilians, when questioned, tell one, with an ominous smile, that the concentrating of troops, etc., enormous supplies in arms and ammunition, are directed against the Ovambos. If that is so, then why are they distant over 1000 English miles from Ovamboland proper, as the crow flies? Placed, in fact, at the extreme opposite corner to the scene of the alleged unrest. As a matter of fact, on visiting the farthest point in southern Ovamboland where the authorities would allow me to go, I found that the Ovambos are by no means a warlike people. All this talk of trouble with the Ovambos is the merest moonshine. Again, not a single black man is allowed the retention of firearms of any kind. All these natives are absolutely unarmed. Police activity is by no means slack, every effort being made to locate any hidden firearms, but nothing is ever found.

A N.C.O. I spoke to declared that a portion of the Ovambos at the extreme northerly part of Amboland, hitherto a mere protectorate whose boundary to this day is undefined, was inhabited by a chief who took a large number of rifles from the Portuguese during the skirmishes in Southern Angola, prior to the Herero trouble with the Germans. But on making official inquiries upon my return to Windhoek later, no one could verify the report. If the Ovambos were really the cause of all this arming to the teeth on the part of the Germans, how is it that the Portuguese trading stations south of the Kunene River are not molested? To-day Portuguese traders may be seen peacefully at work, single-handed, in what is called German territory, and conquering the country by peaceable means. I have had several conversations with both Ovambo leaders and police patrols whilst at Grootfontein North during September of last year. There was nothing which led me to believe that trouble of any sort was brewing.

No. 8.

Windhoek is the capital of German South-West Africa, and one would have thought that there—and not right away down south near the British border—the military centre with supplies would be infinitely greater and on a larger scale. Especially should this be the case when one remembers that it lies some 400 English miles near the "dreaded" Ovamboland. Principally from my own observations conducted on the spot and from information supplied from a trustworthy official source and the ready assistance afforded me by my friend, I found that at the time of my visit a few months since, smiths, farriers, painters, carpenters, and saddlers had more than their hands full in coping with the amount of work thrust on them; saddlers and harnessmakers were, in fact, working overtime at night to satisfy the officers from the various depôts mentioned in the last article, and to supply their wants.....

When completed a great network of railways for strategical purposes leading out to the Union border will be available. To-day mails, say from Lüderitz Bay to Windhoek, are carried by steamer only, a most irregular service. Telegraphic communication, of course, is long established, and many more new branch lines are under construction, under this head. The railway is constructed throughout on the Union pattern, or what is still called the Cape gauge, except the Otawi line, which is narrow gauge, and a small section between Swakopmund and Karibib, half-way to Windhoek, all of which is about to be altered to Cape gauge. Work already has been commenced from the Windhoek side. The Germans hope one day to link up with the South African railways from Kalkfontein South *via* Warmbad, to a point at the border presumably. Thus their troops could be hurried, on the completion of the railways now building, a thousand miles by rail from the north through to the south to the Union border in the space of a few days.

No. 9.

Let me quote a passage which appeared in the columns of the *London Magazine* of March, 1910, signed by "Anglo-German." The writer says, *inter alia :* "During a recent stay in Germany, I was introduced, by a man whom I knew to be one of the chief functionaries of the institute known as the 'Commerce Defence League,' to a friend of his who had just returned from German South-West Africa. On a subsequent meeting I entered into conversation with this gentleman, and made some inquiries concerning the country. He said little headway was made, and little was looked for. Men and money were being freely expended, without present return. The only good harbour was in the hands of the British (Walfisch Bay), as were all the islands on the coast.

"Why, then," I asked, "do the Germans persist in their occupation of the country?"

He answered frankly, smiling craftily: "We Germans look far ahead, my friends. We foresee another *débâcle* in South Africa, and we are on the spot. Thanks to the pioneers of our League, our plans are all matured. The League finance the scheme, and the Government supplies the military forces. Walfisch Bay will before long be German territory, by cession —or otherwise (?), but in the meantime British free trade opposes no obstacles to us, and we can pursue our purpose unmolested."

"What is that purpose?"

"Surely you are not so blind as to need enlightenment?" was his reply. "Germany has long since regarded South Africa as a future possession of her own. When the inevitable happens, and Great Britain finds her hands full elsewhere, we are ready to strike the moment the signal is given, and the Cape, Bechuanaland, Rhodesia—all the frontier States—will fall like ripe apples into our grasp."

I might here state that the Germans are apt to count the unhatched chickens, flushed with the success of their intrigues. Frequently I have heard it stated, whilst in the country, even from Marines, that one day the German ensign would "fly on the Lion's Head," and that in the event of trouble between England and Germany the Boers would side with the invading forces into the Union of South Africa.

INDEX

196 INDEX

Betham-Edwards 105 n
Bethmann - Hollweg (Chancellor)
    178, 180
Bieberstein (Baron Marschall von)
    85, 127
Bismarck 4, 5, 6, 7, 9, 10, 11, 12,
    13, 14, 20, 21, 25, 26, 27, 40,
    44, 50, 66, 87, 92, 93, 94, 95,
    96, 97, 98, 99, 101, 102, 103 n,
    104, 106, 110, 130, 131, 153,
    155, 156, 157, 175
Bloemfontein 60
Blowitz (H. S. de) 8, 98 n
Blücher 3, 21, 186
Blumenthal (Count von) 93 n
Boer Republic 12, 13, 15, 16, 17, 71
Bonn University 33
Bordeaux 94
Bosnia-Herzegovina 85, 115, 119,
    124, 129, 158
Bosphorus 84
Botha (General) 60
Boulanger (General) 100
Bourgeois (M.) 58
Brazil (South) 54, 55, 75, 188
Bremen 12, 13
Brittany 93, 116
Broglie 4 n
Brussels 148, 182
Buchanan (Sir George) 167, 169
Bucher 11, 12, 17
Bucheron (Dr) 37
Bug 160
Bukharest 133, 158
Bulgaria 116, 120, 122, 129, 131,
    132, 135
Bülow (Prince) 59, 72, 128 n
Bundy (Mr) 59
Bunsen (Sir M. de) 164, 165
Burgers (President) 12
Busch 11, 26, 50, 93, 103

Caillaux (Mme.) 140, 165, 166
Calmet (Dom) 110 n
Cambon (Jules) 159, 173, 182
Cameroons 17, 75
Canada 143
Cape Colony 14, 68
Cape Town 17, 143
Carlsbad 127
Carlyle (Thomas) 3, 154

Carthage 142
Cassavetti (Signor) 120 n
Cassel 33
Catherine II 117
Caucasia 82
Central Powers, see also Germany
    and Austria 3, 50, 134, 160, 162,
    167, 168, 169
Ceuta 69
Chamberlain (J.) 19, 58
Charlemagne 103
Charles XII (of Sweden) 44, 139
China 52, 54, 100
Churchill (Winston) 148
Class (Herr) 80 n
Clausewitz 155
Clémenceau 100
Colmar 108
Cologne 77
Congo Free State 52, 147
Constantinople 85, 89, 90, 98, 116,
    117, 121, 126, 127, 133, 172
Crispi 59, 98 n, 131 n
Cromwell (Oliver) 177
Cronstadt 165, 166, 172
Crown Prince 6, 39
Cuba 51
Cyprus 121

Dalny 123
Damascus 88
Daneff 132
Daniell (Herr) 64
Danube 118, 119
Dauphiné 93
Davin (Commandant) 147
Débidour (Mons.) 120 n
Delagoa Bay 13, 15, 57
Delarey (General) 60
Delcassé (Mons.) 69, 70, 71, 77
Demolins (Mons.) 108
Denmark 3
Derby (Lord) 7
Descamps (E.) 176 n
Deschanel (Mons.) 71
Dicey (Edward) 29
Diebitsch 117
Disraeli 66
Döberitz 32
Draga, Queen 136, 170
Durham (Miss Edith) 123, 130

For EU product safety concerns, contact us at Calle de José Abascal, 56–1°,
28003 Madrid, Spain or eugpsr@cambridge.org.

www.ingramcontent.com/pod-product-compliance
Ingram Content Group UK Ltd.
Pitfield, Milton Keynes, MK11 3LW, UK
UKHW012331130625
459647UK00009B/214